THE
QFD
BOOK

THE  BOOK

The Team Approach to Solving Problems and Satisfying Customers Through Quality Function Deployment

Lawrence R. Guinta
Nancy C. Praizler

American Management Association

New York • Atlanta • Boston • Chicago • Kansas City • San Francisco • Washington, D.C.
Brussels • Toronto • Mexico City

This book is available at a special discount when ordered in bulk quantities. For information, contact Special Sales Department, AMACOM, a division of American Management Association, 135 West 50th Street, New York, NY 10020.

This publication is designed to provide accurate and authoritative information in regard to the subject matter covered. It is sold with the understanding that the publisher is not engaged in rendering legal, accounting, or other professional service. If legal advice or other expert assistance is required, the services of a competent professional person should be sought.

AMACOM Books, a division of American Management Association
135 West 50th Street, New York, NY 10020

This book is also distributed by: Quality Resources
A division of The Kraus Organization, Ltd.
One Water Street, White Plains, New York 10601
ISBN 0-527-91726-5

Library of Congress Cataloging-in-Publication Data

Guinta, Lawrence R.
    The QFD book : the team approach to solving problems and
satisfying customers through quality function deployment / Lawrence
R. Guinta, Nancy C. Praizler.
        p.   cm.
    Includes bibliographical references and index.
    ISBN 0-8144-5139-X
    1. Quality function deployment.   2. Production management—Quality
control.   3. New products—Management.   I. Praizler, Nancy C.
II. Title.
TS156.G83   1993   93-9251
658.5'62—dc20   CIP

Printing number

10   9   8   7   6   5   4   3   2   1

We want to dedicate this book to our parents,
Irene and Larry Guinta, Sr.
Over the years their love and example have encouraged us to pursue challenges with confidence. We are successful today because of their
dedication and training.

Contents

Preface

Is your company faced with the strategic issue of introducing a new product or service that may be critical to its survival? Suppose there were a methodology that could tell you the potential success of your options before you tried them. And suppose this methodology could also help you reduce design-to-introduction time by 30 percent while improving quality and lowering overall costs. Interested?

No, it isn't a crystal ball. It is a proven Japanese business methodology called Quality Function Deployment, or QFD.

We are a quality management consulting firm that has conducted over 200 QFD sessions. We've helped aerospace, automotive, manufacturing, and service companies use QFD to solve customer-related problems and design and develop new products and services. From our experience using QFD, we have realized its power and have expanded its application to developing and resolving corporate strategic issues. As a series of questions and matrices QFD is an excellent process for strategic planning and continuous improvement.

QFD has been largely ignored by upper management and nontechnical groups in U.S. business because it's considered too complex. But in this book we've developed a QFD method that is simpler and easier to use. We've field-tested it and have seen employees from all levels of an organization learn it quickly and use it successfully. We want to share this methodology with you—so you can take it with you into the boardroom. We predict that, after using QFD to solve one problem, you'll want to make it a permanent part of your business planning.

If you have questions or comments about our book, please

write to us. Your feedback is part of our continuous improvement process!

Our best wishes for your continued strength in today's marketplace and for success using QFD.

Acknowledgments

No one can write a book without the support of others. We'd like to thank our families and friends for their patience and encouragement while we undertook this endeavor. We missed time with them to sequester ourselves and write about a subject they knew little about. Yet they continually cheered us on and tolerated our preoccupation.

We want also to thank our co-workers for making our absence in the workplace possible. While writing we needed time to immerse ourselves in this work, and leaving our regular jobs was the only way it was possible.

And we want to thank our clients who helped us learn more about QFD. Many of you will recognize examples of work we've done together. Thank you for allowing us to share our joint experience with the readers of our book.

THE QFD BOOK

Introduction:
The Origin and Uses
of QFD

In the late 1960s, Japan became the world's low-cost provider of steel. This tiny island with limited natural resources developed a process to import raw materials and convert them into high-quality steel more cheaply than anyone else could.

As the low-cost producer of steel, Japan focused on further expanding its strategic industrialization into the shipping industry. By the 1970s, the country had captured the title as the world's leading builder of supertanker cargo ships.

Building supertankers is no trivial task. These ships can exceed three football fields in length. Although they are designed to be cavernous for holding cargo, they must utilize sophisticated propulsion, maneuvering, and balance control systems for daily operation. Unlike automobiles, supertankers are not built on a production line. Generally, they are ordered one at a time. Each is unique and may incorporate significant technological advances over the ship built just before it. Most important, each customer purchasing a supertanker has specific cargo-holding requirements. For all these reasons, building a supertanker can be a logistic nightmare.

Many of these supertankers were built by Mitsubishi Heavy Industries at the shipyards in Kobe, Japan. In the late 1960s, Mitsubishi turned to the Japanese government for help in developing the logistics for building these complex cargo ships. The Japanese government contracted with several university professors to create a system that would ensure that each step of the construction process would be linked to fulfilling a specific customer requirement. Thus was born what we call today Quality Function Deployment, or QFD.

A SUCCESSFUL PROCESS IS MADE EVEN BETTER

In 1971, Volkswagen of Germany had just completed a banner year as top import-car manufacturer in the world. In Japan, a fledgling Japanese auto manufacturer wanted to become another Volkswagen. It had introduced its first car in the United States in the mid 1960s. The vehicles were small, and the public initially perceived them as cheap, low-quality economy cars. Part of what led to the public's perception was that the cars rusted more quickly than other cars, especially Volkswagens.

Recognizing the need to quickly change this perception, the Japanese auto manufacturer adapted the process used to build supertankers. First, it set performance benchmarks. The automaker selected three cars as its standards: Fiat, representing the low end; Volkswagen as the target; and Mercedes-Benz as the upper end. The company's research and development tasks were to develop a new painting technique. The first attempt failed; the rust problems did not improve. However, the company did not quit. Instead, it decided not only to change the process but to redesign it.

This company's pickup truck doors had some of the more severe rusting problems, because of the way the doors had been designed and manufactured. Since the doors were small in scale and relatively simple compared to the rest of the vehicle, they provided the company a unique opportunity to try the new methodology adapted from the Kobe shipyards.

To do this, the company needed input from its customers. Small groups of customers—called customer focus groups—were brought in. The company listened to what the customers liked and disliked about the vehicle doors. To its surprise, the company learned things about pickup truck doors it had not previously realized were important. For example, hilly terrain was a concern to customers: When the car was parked downhill, a heavy door was unmanageable for small-framed people, especially women, since it could pull away from them when they opened it. Likewise, closing the door against gravity when inside the truck could be almost impossible.

Parking uphill presented similar problems. Heavy doors made exiting difficult, while entry in the uphill position became a struggle between the occupant and a crushing door. The company learned that customers liked doors with detents—the notches built into the door mechanism that hold them in the open position. However, the detents had to be carefully designed: if too large, movement off the detent was difficult; if too small, they served little useful purpose.

Customers also expressed a preference for how many turns of a window crank it should take to open the window. Rotation should follow some natural ergonomic expectation, as well as have comfortable starting and stopping points. Vent window latches should be openable with one hand, preferably the one closest to the window. And, regardless of their weight, doors should sound solid and heavy.

Using the new QFD methodology, the company was able to capture the voice of its customers. More important, this new system enabled the company to carry its customers' preferences through the engineering and manufacturing processes. By focusing on customer wishes, everyone in the organization had a clearer picture of how his or her job satisfied customers' requirements. The new methodology proved successful for this fledgling Japanese auto manufacturer. With its success on pickup truck doors, Toyota used the system to design other parts of its car. Today, QFD is used extensively for all of its designs.

THE WORD SPREADS

Hearing of this success, other Japanese companies started using QFD methodology. Panasonic pushed it to greater limits, using it not only to understand what its customers wanted at present but to accurately predict what they would want in the future. Witness the company slogan: PANASONIC, JUST SLIGHTLY AHEAD OF OUR TIME.

During the 1970s, Japanese companies continuously improved the QFD methodology and became masters at it. However, it took more than ten years for QFD to reach the United States.

DEFINING QFD

The actual Japanese name for the methodology developed in the Kobe Shipyards is *hin shitsu, ki nou, ten kai*. Translating this into English is difficult because each word has several meanings. For example, *hin shitsu* means "quality," "features," "qualities," or "attributes." *Ki nou* means "function" or "mechanization." And the closest words we have for *ten kai* are *diffusion, development, deployment,* or *evolution* (see Figure I-1).*

When U.S. companies became aware of QFD, the country was in the midst of a "quality" revolution. Most major industries were looking for ways to improve the quality of their products. Indeed, QFD is a powerful tool to help an organization provide higher-quality products and services more efficiently and at reduced cost.

Quality Function Deployment is a misleading name for an excellent tool. It is great for problem solving, decision making, and planning. Unfortunately, over the years QFD has been tagged with a variety of other names, such as the Voice of the Customer, the House of Quality, Customer-Driven Engineering, Matrix Product Planning, and Decision Matrix. All attempts to change the name have only enforced its original translation.

---

*According to Aki Kumayama, professor at Thunderbird College of the American Graduate School of International Management in Phoenix, Arizona, it is very difficult to determine whether a noun in Japanese is singular or plural. The number is usually determined by the context. For this reason, *hin shitsu* may refer to quality or qualities. *Ki nou* (pronounced *key-know*) may mean either function or functions. *Ten kai* may mean development or developments. When the Japanese refer to quality control, they often use the phrase "total quality control," or TQC.

Figure I-1. QFD name in Japanese.

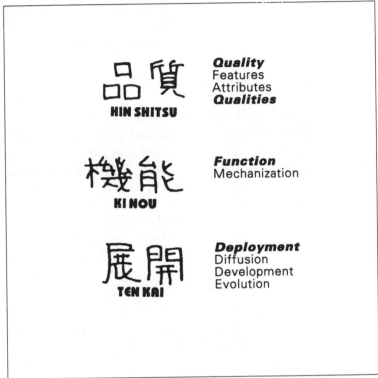

Quality Function Deployment is a pointed way of listening to customers to learn exactly what they want, and then using a logical system to determine how best to fulfill those needs with available resources. QFD is a team builder. It ensures that everyone works together to give customers exactly what they want. Likewise, it gives everyone in the organization a road map showing how every step from design through delivery interacts to fulfill customer requirements.

Another way of viewing QFD is by answering three questions:

1. What are the *qualities* the customer desires? (A quality product or service is an absolute and is assumed.)

2. What *function(s)* must this product serve and what functions must we use to provide this product or service?
3. Based upon the resources we have available, how can
   we *best provide* what our customer wants?

WHAT QFD DOES

Quality Function Deployment takes broad product specifications or specific problems and, through a series of matrices,
breaks them into specific action assignments. These assignments set the minimum level of effort that must be made to
satisfy the customer. In short, QFD translates customer requirements into appropriate technical requirements. It helps
teams determine the correct methods, tools, and order of use.
The QFD process can be used by both product- and service-
based companies. It is an essential tool in implementing Total
Quality Management (TQM). QFD is a low to medium technology that brings out the best in high-tech tools and methodologies.

THE BENEFITS OF QFD

The word *quality* is one we use often. Whether describing a
product or service, we frequently refer to something as being
of high quality. But when it comes to defining *quality*, no two
descriptions are the same. In fact, we find everyone in business
struggles for a clear, concise definition of *quality*.

The description we think best defines *quality* is the following: (1) fulfills requirements; (2) is on time; and (3) is within
costs. Quality, like beauty, is in the eye of the beholder.
Whether you are developing a product or a service, quality is
whatever your customer considers it to be. QFD ensures that
you fulfill your customer's definition of quality. It does this by
providing several benefits.

Shorter Development Cycles

QFD is a system for placing development efforts at the front of
a program rather than at the end. With development up-front,

your team can focus on planning and problem prevention. This is the area in which the Japanese feel Western society fails miserably, best exemplified by "fire fighting" manufacturing teams that have to cure problems which could have been avoided in the first place.

None of the Traditional Tradeoffs

U.S. companies and customers have grown accustomed to facing tradeoffs, most commonly between quality, time, and cost. The model we've come to accept is that these entities must be in conflict with each other. We have come to believe that we cannot have one of these features without giving up another.

For example, we generally think that quality can be improved if we spend more money. Costs can be lowered if we cheapen the product or process. Or we can get to market sooner if we omit certain steps or spend more money. But through their successful use of QFD, the Japanese realize that these tradeoffs do not need to be. They optimize their products and the process design; they maximize performance while reducing variation and waste. Manufacturing processes are structured so as to be desensitized to variations caused by operators, equipment, and materials; the product performs well within a wide range of usage. As a result, the product is usually easier to make, less expensive, and of high quality.

Lower Costs, Greater Productivity

In an effort to maintain quality, we in the United States commonly specify many internal requirements and assign each high importance. We try to design and build to specification tolerances, and continually manage around the tolerance stackup. When problems occur, we react to them.

In contrast, the Japanese decide what is important, then design and build target values to reduce variation and waste while optimizing product and process design. As a result, they experience fewer design changes and start-up problems, along with improved quality and reliability. By optimizing the design of both product and process, they often see considerable cost savings.

We have seen many claims for QFD about the time and money saved, along with enormous increases in productivity. When we first became familiar with QFD several years ago, these claims seemed exaggerated—too good to be true. However, after working with many different manufacturing and serviced-based companies in the United States, we have commonly experienced a 50 percent reduction in overall costs. We have seen companies reduce their project times by one third, and we have helped companies achieve 200 percent increases in productivity!

CHANGING YOUR THINKING

In this book we discuss paradigms. A *paradigm* is a model of how something is normally done. QFD is a paradigm shift from traditional *manufacturing* quality control to *product* design quality control.

Traditional manufacturing quality control is achieved through inspecting physical products—by observing and measuring them. This procedure is commonly referred to as inspected-in quality. QFD helps a company shift from inspecting products to designing quality into its products.

For instance, in the design phase, QFD involves many intangibles long before the design becomes lines on paper. This is the stage when quality is designed into the product, service, or process. Designed-in quality is the foundation for simultaneous or concurrent engineering.

Developments in the television industry are an example of designed-in quality vs. manufacturing quality control. In the 1950s and 1960s, television sets used vacuum tubes to perform the various electronic functions. The reliability of these tubes was poor, and many of us can remember having the local television repairman over one evening to fix the set. He would pull the TV out from the wall, remove the back, and identify any tube that did not glow red when the set was turned on. If the problem was more severe, he would open his heavy metal toolbox and reveal what appeared to be, for that era, a sophisticated electronic diagnostic instrument. As he proceeded with his diagnostics, we hoped the problem was only a tube or simple adjustment that could be made quickly, so we could finish our favorite program. If the repairman could not solve the problem, then he would cart the set off to the shop for several days, where it would be repaired and tested.

In the late 1960s, television manufacturers began using solid state semiconductors, more commonly known as transistors. Transistors allowed manufacturers to dramatically reduce the size of circuits, and as a result, entire circuits could be fitted onto cards approximately 4 by 6 inches in size. These new printed circuit cards, as they came to be known, opened up new possibilities for electronic equipment manufacturers. Quasar was one of the first companies to incorporate transistor technology into its models. In an effort to reduce repair costs and downtime, Quasar engineers took advantage of the new technology.

Repairing televisions was a difficult and laborious task. It required physically moving the set to gain access to the back. But besides being difficult, it was dangerous because the repairman was exposed to the high voltage that operated the picture tube. To make the repair task easier, quicker, and less costly, the engineers designed the circuit cards to be plugged in through a hidden panel in front of the television. Marketing people loved the idea and were able to sell the Quasar television as the set with the "works in a drawer."

Although this innovation simplified repairs, it did little to improve the quality of the television set. The Quasar paradigm was to make the set easier to repair when it broke—this is traditional manufacturing quality control. While still in the factory, each Quasar set experienced, on average, four problems each. But at this same time in Japan, televisions were being designed to avoid needing repair—this is designed-in quality. A few years after introduction of the Quasar set, a Japanese company purchased Quasar. It kept the work force, but fired many of the company's managers. By using QFD, the new management was able to reduce quality defects over the next two years to only four problems per 100 sets!

Quite simply, QFD works. It is an important tool to have in your company's toolbox. Like any other tool, you do not use it for every job; however, for the right application, few methods can match it. QFD helps teams systematically reach consensus on:

- What to do
- The best ways to do it
- The best order in which to accomplish it
- The staffing and resources required

QFD breaks down functional barriers and replaces emotion with logic. It allows representatives from multiple disciplines or departments to develop solutions. And it results in solutions that bring about a quality product or service.

It is also an excellent meeting format for problem solving. Providing a unique format for capturing meeting minutes, the QFD model allows team members to review and recall exact details months and even years after a meeting. Thus, the QFD documentation process is a highly effective way for getting new members up to speed on what to do and why.

1

The QFD Business Strategy

Quality Function Deployment is a simple and logical methodology involving a set of matrices. These matrices help determine exactly what the customer wants, how well the competition is satisfying the customer, and where unfulfilled niches exist in the marketplace. They also help decide if a company has the resources to successfully enter these niche markets and what the minimum quality levels are. In short, the customer's product or service requirements become the specifications for giving the customer exactly what he or she wants.

WAYS TO USE QFD

An excellent tool for strategic planning, QFD simplifies strategic thinking with a framework for clarifying and meeting goals. For the decision maker, it helps identify what is important by providing a logical system to replace emotion-based decision making. For instance, the QFD methodology helps bring together diverse data from many sources—specific customer expectations, customer surveys, competitive market analyses, engineering expertise, manufacturing capabilities, company resources, strategic goals, and cost considerations.

The uniqueness of this methodology is that these data can be captured and statistically evaluated in the initial days of decision making. This is when decisions are made on the probability of success and whether to proceed with product or service development. By using collective knowledge, the company can identify what will work, what will not work, and what things should be avoided. Since up to 80 percent of a project's cost is locked in during this early phase, this early assessment can greatly reduce program costs and development time.

The QFD model presents these data in a side-by-side format showing relationships, correlations, or conflicts. In some cases, it shows where tradeoffs exist between product requirements and current resources. The analysis of large amounts of data is made easier and logical. If you decide to go into a venture, the minimum quality levels that must be achieved will already be defined.

QFD is also ideal for shifting to Total Quality Management (TQM). Companies such as Ford and General Motors now believe that QFD is vital for implementing TQM.[1] QFD is especially helpful in initially sorting out the systems, procedures, and products or services to address first. Then subsequent QFDs are performed by cross-functional teams on each product or problem.

QFD can be a visual plan for the company showing the linkage between departments and helping everyone understand how his or her work contributes to satisfying the customer. It helps eliminate errors and miscommunications by graphically clarifying objectives, interactions, and tasks.

As a company gains experience using QFD, the model becomes historical information for continuous improvement. The data can be used for product revisions or for introducing new products or services. And it helps teams pinpoint the tools to use, such as Taguchi methods or Design of Experiments. The QFD matrices become references for determining progress and success and identifying areas where future adjustments need to be made. In short, the matrix generated by QFD serves as a roadmap showing where the team wants to go and the milestones it must pass to arrive at its destination.

QFD is also a highly effective way of capturing information from meetings. It converts data into a graphic representation— a single-page QFD matrix is equivalent to many pages of written documentation. When new members join a team, they can quickly see team goals and progress, as well as what their specific contributions must be.

SPECIFIC APPLICATIONS

QFD has been successfully used by both product- and service-based companies. The Japanese have used it in the manufacture of automobiles, "electronics, home appliances, clothing, integrated circuits, synthetic rubber, construction equipment, and agricultural engines."[2] They have also used it to design retail outlets and develop apartment layouts, and for services such as swimming pools and schools.

In the United States, QFD has been used to establish supplier development criteria, develop RFP/RFQ systems, and prepare for the Malcolm Baldrige Award. Companies have called upon QFD to help them improve service, create training programs, select new employees, and design new products and services.

Let's look at a particular use of QFD. Thiokol Strategic Operations builds solid rocket motors for Strategic and Tactical weapons systems, ordnance items, and related products. As part of its continuous improvement effort, Thiokol wanted to improve its ability to measure and certify the companies that supplied parts. It began work on a supplier certification program. This program had been under development for many months, but was not proceeding according to expectations. Thiokol asked us to help them analyze and redesign their program.

We introduced QFD. Over the course of two weeks, more than thirty people representing every departmental function participated in a series of QFD sessions to determine the important qualities of a supplier and their relative importance. Thiokol used Pareto analysis to sort the suppliers according to potential impact and QFD to analyze each supplier in relation to Thiokol's needs. On the basis of those findings, Thiokol organized a sequential list of suppliers to assess. The QFD process greatly reduced this development time and provided a superior program.

Thiokol's new program is called Achieving Certified Excellence (ACE). Today, many feel that Thiokol's ACE program is a model not only for the aerospace industry but for all industries wishing to improve relationships with suppliers. Ford and General Motors are using QFD and request that their suppliers do the same.[3]

More Efficient Product Development

Companies using QFD for product development have experienced a 50 percent reduction in costs, 33 percent reduction in development time, and 200 percent increase in productivity. For instance, using QFD, Toyota and Honda have been able to release new products every 3.5 years—in contrast to U.S. auto companies, which need 5 years to bring new products to market.[4]

But QFD is also a preventive methodology, suggesting the probability of success or failure. For example, suppose a company wants to add infrared-optic-global positioning technology to its new surface-to-air missile. Although the company has good experience in this field, it uses QFD to identify potential long-term problems that could delay or even cripple the program. It also uses QFD to determine which items require new technology, or are high in risk. Then it compares this list to its resources and capabilities, discovering a critical problem that could occur in manufacturing. As a result, it may change its plan and use a different technology. By using QFD and tapping the collective knowledge of the organization, the company is able to foresee and avoid costly development problems.

QFD identifies necessary changes *before* they are a design on paper. From our experience, we estimate that 80 percent of overall costs are locked in during the design phase; the remaining 20 percent occur during manufacturing or implementation. Yet companies consistently rush products into production, spending enormous amounts of money to reduce manufacturing costs. QFD was developed as a method of catching as many design flaws as possible—early in the process. Although some still get through, we typically find that larger problems are caught long before the project gets started. As a result, only about 30 percent of the normal changes must be done (see Figure 1-1).

Let's look at another example. A company had assigned development and installation of a manufacturing system to a seven-person team. The team had fourteen months to complete the project. After working ten months on the design, the team hit an impasse.

We helped the team do a two-day QFD to evaluate its past ten-month effort. QFD clarified what had to be done to complete the project and resolve the impasse. The team completed the remaining four months' work in eight days. Thus, the organization realized a 29 percent reduction in implementation time and an estimated $32,000 savings in personnel costs.

Figure 1-1.   Paradigm shifts: QFD vs. traditional U.S. business methodologies.

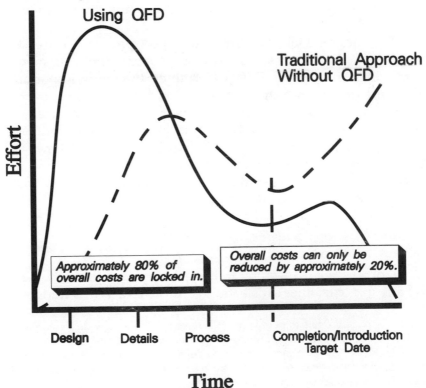

When QFD is not used in product development, there is a surge in complaints immediately following start-up. This adds to the cost of nonconformance.[5] But by using QFD, this surge disappears because the team has anticipated the problems and eliminated them.

Improved Product Quality and Reliability

QFD is one of the best systems to solve complex, multipart business problems, primarily by using people from different disciplines and with different perspectives. Indeed, QFD requires and encourages the use of multidisciplinary teams.* It provides a natural process to break down functional barriers and improve communication. Often, employee satisfaction is improved as well, because employees enjoy working in concert rather than in conflict. When employees see success and quality in their work, they feel pride and commitment to the company.

In a sense, QFD measures how one problem relates to another. Using simple statistics, it summarizes the team members' different perspectives, determines the most important elements of the problem, and indicates how they can best be solved. The result is a new approach to old, "unsolvable" problems. For example, in the Introduction, we described Toyota's experience with QFD in the late 1960s. At that time, its rust warranty costs exceeded company profit by a factor of 4.[6] Elimination of the rust during the warranty period was achieved only after Toyota used QFD.

Greater Customer Satisfaction

QFD forces the organization to keep its focus on the customer. As a result, customer satisfaction is improved. When tradeoffs

---

Multidisciplinary refers to people from different disciplines within an organization. It is similar to cross-functional or cross-departmental, however it is more inclusive. For example, within each department, you may have a variety of different disciplines. General Motors' "Targets for Excellence" program uses this word because it is all-encompassing.

are necessary, they are made to the customer's advantage—not the engineer's or the manufacturing department's.

QFD helps reduce the number of sales calls necessary to define the customer's requirements. For instance, specific requirements are listed on the QFD matrix, after having been gathered through market research and customer focus groups. Though these requirements are originally in the customer's words, such as "quieter ride" or "easier to handle," the team translates the statements into design characteristics, such as more insulation, slower motor speed, or less weight. In the process, the customer requirements are prioritized, helping the team focus on the most important items. Thus QFD helps create a superiority difference between companies in the customer's mind. For instance, Toyota, Panasonic, and Sony became successful by listening to their customers' needs and offering products that met those needs. As they became more experienced, they were able to predict what customers would want!

In a similar vein, customers may be internal as well as external. Internal customers are people within the organization next in line to receive the product or service. They often add value to the previous person's work. QFD helps quickly determine who the internal customers are. Including these internal customers on the project team helps identify their requirements, but in cases when this is not practical, QFD research techniques can identify those requirements.

QFD is a proven system to solicit customer feedback. The competitive assessment of the QFD model uses market research to indicate how satisfied customers are with each product characteristic. This assessment also shows how the company rates relative to its competitors for each product characteristic.

Lastly, QFD can help a company develop long-term partnerships with its customers. When customers are included in the development process, they take interest in the outcome. Because of their involvement, they want the product to succeed. Also, since QFD gives customers information about the product's development, they can make a more rational decision when comparing the competition.

Better Proposals and Quotations

QFD greatly reduces the effort required to respond to labor-intensive and costly requests for proposal and quotation (RFPs and RFQs). RFPs typically do not convey information that is critical to satisfying customer needs. While appearing to be specific and providing product or service requirements in great detail, they often do not list qualities most needed, nor prioritize them. Also, they rarely define the feature tradeoffs prospective customers are willing to make.

QFD has helped companies determine which RFPs to respond to (see Case Study 2 in Chapter 9). It has also helped them identify which type of new business matches their strategic objectives and available resources, so that they now focus only on RFPs that directly relate to their corporate goals. The percentage of winning RFPs increases because the products or services are well matched with the client's requirements. Some companies believe that they must respond to 100 RFPs to win 20, but companies using QFD win the same 20 contracts by responding to only 25 RFPs: an increase in win ratio from 20 to 80 percent!

In addition, these companies are sometimes awarded business without even responding to an RFP. Instead, they conduct a QFD session with the prospective client to not only identify specific requirements but also help the client prioritize them. The company gains an advantage over competitors who only respond to the RFP, and increases its chances of winning the contract.

A large aerospace contractor was in the midst of implementing QFD when it received a request for proposal regarding a major piece of new business. The RFP was thousands of pages long; rather than respond in its normal fashion, the company decided to use QFD. Marketing and engineering teams worked to determine if the new business proposal strategically fit the company. Deciding that it did, they created a list of basic requirements as stated in the client's RFP. They invited the prospective client—a branch of the armed forces—for a QFD session.

At first the client refused—the meeting would give the

aerospace contractor an unfair advantage. However, the client was a proponent of Total Quality Management and believed in the need to develop partnerships with suppliers. In the TQM approach, QFD is a vital component. The team convinced the client that the competition should be doing the same thing. Finally, the client agreed to the session.

During the QFD session, the client was asked to list the important elements of the proposal. At first, the client referred to the "book" (the RFP), saying that everything was clearly stated there. But the RFP list was reduced to twelve major items by asking the client to describe the *qualities* wanted.

The company representatives then prioritized the list by asking the client:

> If we can only accomplish one of these items for you, which one should it be?

The client struggled to answer this question, finally agreeing on the most important item. Then, the client was asked the following question for the remaining eleven items:

> If we find we are capable of accomplishing an additional item, which one should we complete?

Again, the client struggled, only after a lengthy time deciding which item was second most important. This process was repeated for the remaining items. Halfway through the first day, the client said:

> Defining what we really want is difficult. Prioritizing the list is even tougher. We have never been asked to do this before. Coming in here, we thought we knew what we wanted. But going through this process, we realize that we have some tough answers to come up with when we get back home. We have never done this before. . . . Do you think we could take a copy of this list back home with us?

The aerospace contractor won the contract. Instead of guessing about what was most important, it knew because its client had identified the critical items. When it wrote its proposal, it focused on those critical requirements and was able to offer features the competitors didn't know were needed.

MAKING A PARADIGM SHIFT

Customer satisfaction is imperative for long-term business survival, as we all know. Total Quality Management and continuous improvement philosophies are instrumental in achieving this. And both philosophies require new tools such as QFD, which involve a new way of thinking, or a paradigm shift.

A paradigm is a model of how something is done. Adopting TQM and using QFD require a major paradigm shift. The old paradigm is quality control inspection of products after they are produced; as mentioned in the Introduction, this is *inspected-in* quality. The new paradigm is to design quality into the products and their manufacturing processes so that products are produced error-free; this is referred to as *designed-in* quality. QFD has an unmatched ability to help companies design in their quality.

This same paradigm shift applies to strategic business planning. Some companies develop goals and then hope they can implement a strategy to achieve them; this is the same as inspected-in quality in the manufacturing process. Rather, a company today must determine and formulate the strategy it needs to achieve its goals; this is the equivalent of designed-in quality. A paradigm shift will move a company to make strategic business decisions based upon a designed-in quality approach.

TRADEOFFS

A business is constantly faced with tradeoff decisions regarding quality, time, and cost. When deciding to improve quality, a tradeoff often is necessary. Traditionally, the following considerations have influenced tradeoff decisions:

1. Product quality can be improved only if a company spends more money.
2. Product cost can be lowered if the product or process is cheapened.
3. A product can be brought to market sooner if certain steps are omitted, or if more money is spent to speed up certain operations.

These tradeoffs have become second nature; we think of them as "the law of nature." Yet there are alternative methods for addressing these conflicts between quality, time, and cost. Japanese and U.S. manufacturers historically have taken different approaches.

U.S. Approach

Americans follow a design philosophy that consists of the following three principles:

1. Everything is important.
2. Manage the tolerance stackup.
3. React to customer problems.

The traditional approach is that everything is important; believing this we think helps ensure that quality is designed into the product. As a result, we design and build to specification tolerances and continuously manage around something called the *tolerance stackup.*

For example, a rifle consists of various different parts. In many cases, each part may be produced by a different supplier. Yet when all the parts are assembled, the rifle must function properly and safely. If we were making a single rifle, we could customize the individual parts to fit together. However, for parts to be randomly interchangeable, we must control the specifications and tolerances for each part. For example, the rifle barrel may work well with a .500-inch inside diameter bore. In testing, a tolerance of .495 to .505 works well. However, for the barrel to function with a variety of parts made by different suppliers, the tolerance may have to be limited to .499 to .501 inch.

Here is where tolerance stackup comes in. The designers attempt to keep tolerances close on all critical parts. In many cases, actual tolerances are significantly tighter than what is really needed. However, in order for suppliers to make the parts, they must have some tolerance on each of their dimensions. Using this technique, if the manufacturer of the barrel is on the low side of the allotted tolerance, and the maker of the bolt is on the high side, the rifle will still function properly: A designed-in ability to handle mismatched parts has been created. Because the rifle can work with looser tolerances, the tighter ones specified (.499 to .501 inch) increase the manufacturing cost. Thus, higher cost results from an attempt to improve quality.

When the tolerance stackup does not work, there are problems. If one supplier does not maintain control, there could be *out-of-tolerance* parts. The rifle may still assemble properly; however, it may malfunction or injure someone owing to its out-of-tolerance components.

Japanese Approach

The Japanese follow three different principles in their manufacturing:

1. Decide what is important.
2. Design to reduce variation.
3. Optimize the product.

They start by using QFD to decide what is really important. In the case of the rifle, QFD defines what tolerances are truly needed. QFD further predicts what tolerances can cause potential process and product failures.

With QFD output, the Japanese design and build target values to reduce variation and waste. By recognizing in advance what features and tolerances will be difficult to maintain, they work with suppliers and internal processes to modify the design so as to head off potential problems. As a result, many of their products are easier and less costly to produce.

Finally, the Japanese optimize their product and process design. That is, they continuously improve their products and processes to lower costs and improve quality. Their manufacturing process becomes desensitized to variation from equipment, operators, and materials. The result is a product and process that performs well under a wide range of usages and that uses components which are more compatible during manufacturing. While the methodology may seem to have only minor differences from the U.S. method, Japanese success with QFD has had a major impact on the United States.

NOTES

1. *Harvard Business Review*, May 1988, p. 63. Also General Motors, "Targets for Excellence" program, and Ford Motor Company, "Total Quality Excellence" program.
2. *Harvard Business Review*, May 1988, p. 63.
3. General Motors, "Targets for Excellence" program, and Ford Motor Company, "Total Quality Excellence" program.
4. *Automotive Industries*, July 1987, p. 21.
5. P. B. Crosby, *Quality Is Free* (New York: McGraw-Hill, 1979).
6. *Quality Function Deployment*, Executive Briefing Ver. 2.1 (Dearborn, Mich.: American Supplier Institute, Inc., 1989), pp. 2–7.

2

The QFD System and the Customer

Quality Function Deployment, or QFD, is a methodology that helps teams make decisions. When using this methodology a team develops a QFD model that consists of the following parts:

1. An *Objective Statement*, a description of the goal, problem, or objective of the team effort.
2. The *Whats*, a list of characteristics of a product, process, or service, as defined by customers.
3. *Importance Ratings*, or weighted values assigned the *Whats* indicating relative importance.
4. A *Correlation Matrix* which shows the relationship between the *Hows*.
5. The *Hows*, or ways of achieving the *Whats*.
6. *Target Goals*, indicators of whether the team wants to increase or decrease a *How*, or set a target value for it.
7. A *Relationship Matrix*, a systematic means for identifying the level of relationship between a product/service characteristic (*What*) and a way to achieve it (*How*).
8. *Customer Competitive Assessment*, a review of competitive products/service characteristics in comparison with the team's product or service.
9. *Technical Competitive Assessment* or *How Muches*, the company's engineering specifications for each *How* and the competitor's technical specifications.

10. *Probability Factors*, values indicating the ease with which the company could achieve each *How*.
11. *Absolute Score*, the sum of the calculated values for each *How* or column in the *Relationship Matrix*.
12. *Relative Score*, a sequential numbering of each *How* according to its *Absolute Score*. Number one is entered for the *How* with the highest score, two for the next highest, and so on.

Figure 2-1 shows the parts of the QFD model.

THE FOUR PHASES OF QFD

Like a roadmap, the four phases of QFD are a guide through the product development cycle from product design to production. The four phases are (1) design, (2) details (may be referred to as parts), (3) process, and (4) production. These phases help communicate product requirements from the customers to the design teams to the production operators (see Figure 2-2).

Each phase has a matrix consisting of a vertical column of *Whats* and a horizontal row of *Hows*. *Whats* are customer requirements; *Hows* are ways of achieving them. At each stage, the *Hows* that are most important, require new technology, or are of high risk to the organization are carried to the next phase.

1. *Design*. In the design phase, the customer helps define the product or service requirements. The QFD matrix helps the team translate customer needs into *Whats*. After the *Whats* are determined, the team begins developing the matrix. The team creates different ways of achieving the requirements—these become the *Hows*. After further evaluation, some of the *Hows* will be carried to the next phase.

2. *Details*. The *Hows* carried over from phase 1 become the *Whats* for the second phase. Here, the details and components necessary to produce the product or service are determined. The details emerging from this phase have the strongest rela-

Figure 2-1.   Components of the QFD model.

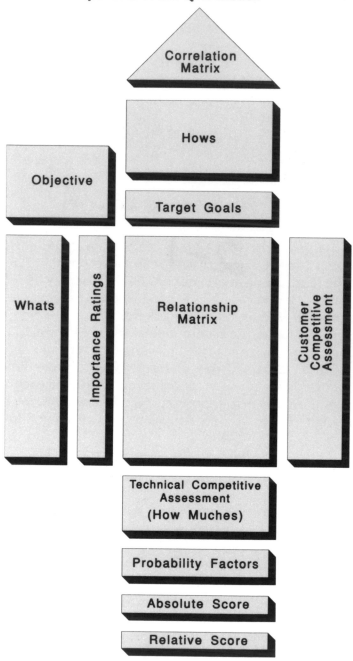

Figure 2-2. The four phases of QFD.

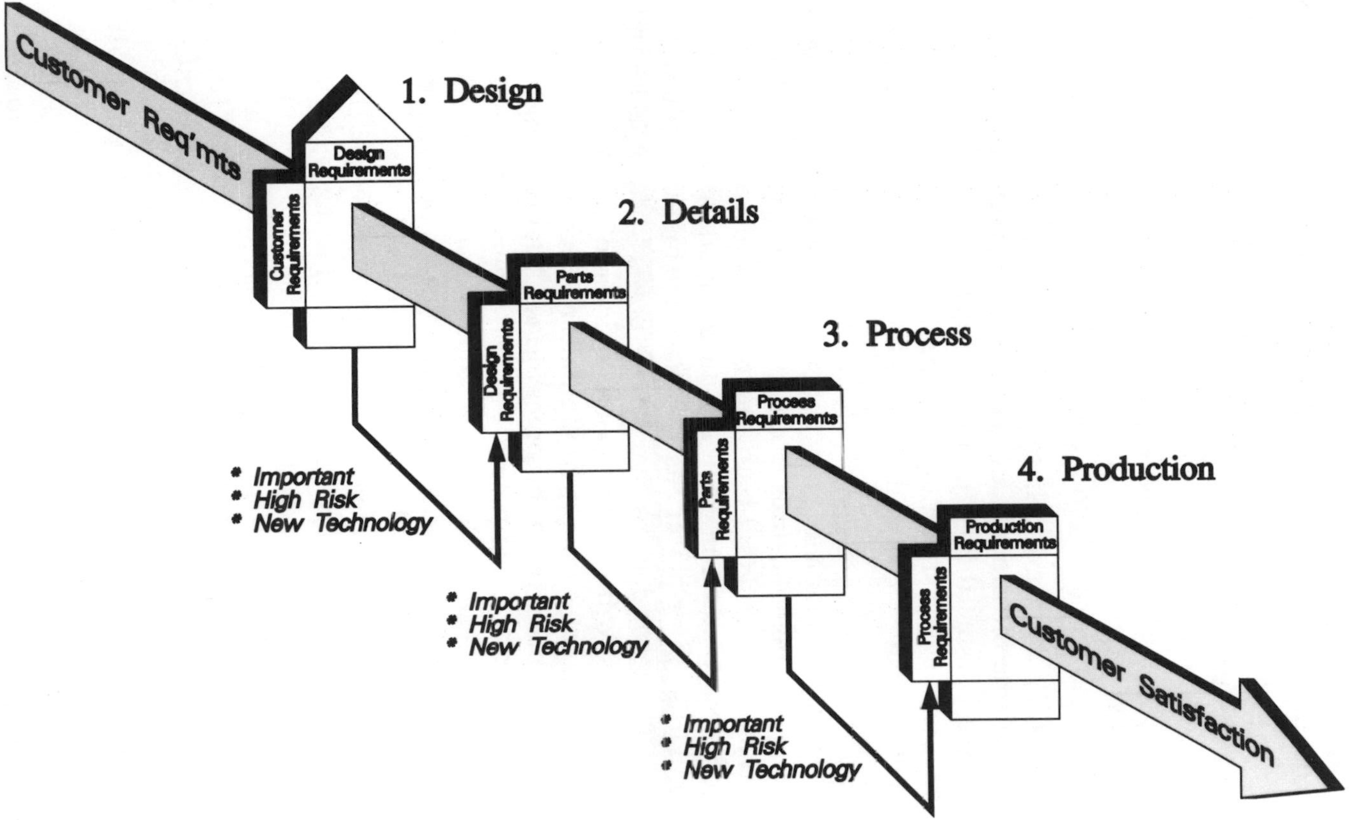

1. Design   2. Details   3. Process   4. Production

Customer Req'mts

Customer Requirements
Design Requirements

Design Requirements
Parts Requirements

Parts Requirements
Process Requirements

Process Requirements
Production Requirements

Customer Satisfaction

* Important
* * High Risk
* * * New Technology

* Important
* * High Risk
* * * New Technology

* Important
* * High Risk
* * * New Technology

tionship to fulfilling the product requirements specified by the customer. They are the *Hows* carried over to the next phase.

3. *Process.* In the third phase, a matrix is developed showing the processes required to produce the product. The *Hows* from the second phase become the *Whats* for this third matrix. The processes that emerge in this phase will best fulfill the product requirements specified by the customer. They are the *Hows* that are carried to the fourth phase.

4. *Production.* In phase 4, the production requirements for producing the product are developed. The *Hows* from the third phase become the *Whats* in this final phase. The production methods determined now will enable the company to produce a high-quality product that meets the customer's requirements.

As an example of how the four phases work, suppose your company manufactures power tools. You discover that your professional building-trade customers want your current drill to be more powerful. Your organization takes this information and lists "more power" as a *What* on the matrix in phase 1.

The team decides that "more power" can be achieved in three ways: with a larger motor, a different motor technology, or a different winding configuration. Each of these ways of achieving more power becomes a *How*. After creating a *Correlation Matrix* and computing the cell values in the *Relationship Matrix,* the team finds that the larger motor will best satisfy the customer's requiremens. "Larger motor" is now transferred to the phase 2 matrix, where it becomes a *What.*

In the second phase the team determines the important details or parts of a larger motor by creating a second QFD model. By doing a *Technical Assessment* and computing the values in the *Relationship Matrix,* it decides that the most critical component of any larger motor design is the shaft of the motor itself. The engineer's input into the *Technical Assessment* helps the team recognize that maintaining the current shaft size will save the cost of redesigning the entire drill. "Motor shaft" is entered into the matrix as a *How.* It then is transferred to the phase 3 matrix.

In phase 3, the team evaluates different ways to improve

the shaft's ability to handle the higher torque produced by the larger motor. The team members determine they can achieve this by using a different material and heat-treating process. They reached this conclusion by consulting with engineers during the *Technical Assessment.* "Material" and "heat treating" are entered on the matrix as *Hows.* The information is then carried forward to the phase 4 matrix.

In the fourth phase, the team determines how to make the new shaft and assemble the motor. It determines that either of two different production solutions can be used to manufacture the new motor assembly: modify several pieces of existing equipment or purchase a single new machine tool. Even though the new machine is more expensive, the team selects that option because it best fulfills the customer's requirements. See Figure 2-3 for a schematic or the whole process.

One of the strengths of QFD is that, throughout the phases, everyone is able to assess how the solutions would help satisfy customer requirements. Even in the fourth phase, involving selection of manufacturing equipment, all decisions are based on achieving the highest level of customer satisfaction. When a decision is made, it is made to the customer's advantage, not the engineering or manufacturing department's. The customer perspective overrides department preferences.

As mentioned in Chapter 1, the four phases of QFD break down the functional barriers between departments in the organization. But navigating through these four phases requires commitment and diligence, as well as strong team leadership and dedicated members. As John Hauser and Don Clausing said in an article written for *The Harvard Business Review,* "None of this is simple. [This] . . . elegant idea ultimately decays into process, and processes will be confounding as long as human beings are involved. But that is no excuse to hold back."[1]

TYPES OF CUSTOMERS

QFD methodology is based on the philosophy that products and services should be designed according to customer re-

Figure 2-3. Implementing the four phases of QFD.

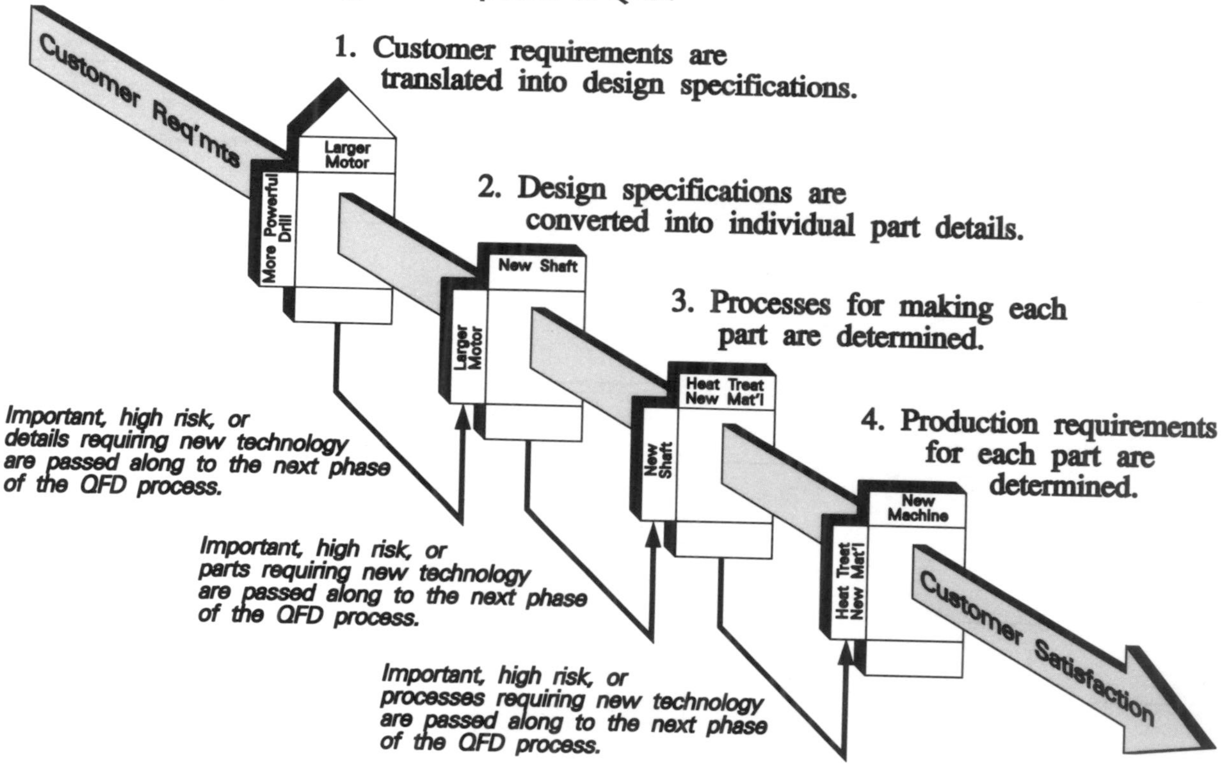

1. Customer requirements are translated into design specifications.

2. Design specifications are converted into individual part details.

3. Processes for making each part are determined.

4. Production requirements for each part are determined.

Customer Req'mts

Customer Satisfaction

More Powerful Drill

Larger Motor

Larger Motor

New Shaft

New Shaft

Heat Treat New Mat'l

Heat Treat New Mat'l

New Machine

Important high risk, or details requiring new technology are passed along to the next phase of the QFD process.

Important high risk, or parts requiring new technology are passed along to the next phase of the QFD process.

Important high risk, or processes requiring new technology are passed along to the next phase of the QFD process.

quirements. Therefore, the customer is the most important part of the process.

There are different types of customers, each with unique needs and wants. It's important that the team know which customer perspective it needs in each of the four phases, so as to include the right customer at the right time.

There are three types of customers: (1) internal, (2) intermediate, and (3) external (see Figure 2-4).

1. *Internal customers.* Those within the organization who are next in line to receive the product or service are internal customers. They may be production line people who assemble the product or service representatives who help customers use the product or service.
2. *Intermediate customers.* A business's intermediate customers are often distributors or middlepersons. They buy the product and sell it to retailers. They have special distribution needs and know what their customers want. A company's ability to meet those needs will determine how well the distributor sells the product. Intermediate customers are an important group whose needs must be considered in product design and production.
3. *External customers.* The consumer of the product or service is the external customer. His or her needs are the most important, because the individual will not buy the product or service if it doesn't meet expectations and requirements. If these customers do not buy the product, then intermediate customers will not buy it either.

For example, if you are designing a new power drill for the commercial marketplace, construction workers are the external customers, power-tool distributors are the intermediate customers, and the manufacturing group is your internal customer. Though some needs are similar, each group of customers has different concerns. The construction workers (external customers) are concerned with product performance, durability, weight, comfort, and ergonomics. The distributors (inter-

Figure 2-4.   Types of customers.

Internal Customers

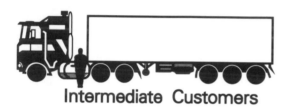

Intermediate Customers

External Customers

mediate customers) share interest in those product characteristics, but are also concerned with delivery, pricing, and
availability. The manufacturing group (internal customers)
shares these concerns, however, it has a unique list of its own.
They are concerned about whether they'll be able to manufacture and assemble the power drill within cost and to specifica-

tions. They are concerned that company designers will create product designs that are costly or inefficient to assemble, or that will require later changes that could be avoided.

LEVELS OF CUSTOMER REQUIREMENTS

There are four levels of customer requirements. Your company must satisfy the requirements of each level before addressing those of the next. The four levels are (1) Expecters, (2) Spokens, (3) Unspokens, and (4) Exciters (see Figure 2-5).

1. *Expecters.* The basic qualities you must offer to be competitive and remain in business are Expecters. These are characteristics customers assume as part of the product or service. Customers rarely ask about them, because they expect them as standard features.

For example, when you buy a new car, you assume it meets all Department of Transportation (DOT) minimum safety requirements. You don't ask the salesperson to see the DOT certification. Similarly, when you buy a new home, you assume that it meets all local, city, and federal building codes. Customers expect a company's products and services to meet minimum requirements. When they don't, customers take their business to the competitors, who can fulfill basic quality expectations.

2. *Spokens.* Specific features customers say they want in a product or service are Spokens. They are items a company is willing to provide to satisfy its customer. Spokens are usually communicated verbally or in writing. Purchase orders, contracts, and requests for proposal are ways Spokens are communicated by customers. For example, when a family looks for a new home, it may specify verbally or in writing the square footage requirements, the number of bedrooms or bathrooms, and color and fixture preferences.

3. *Unspokens.* Product or service characteristics customers don't talk about are Unspokens. Though silent, they are important and cannot be ignored. It is the team's job to discover

Figure 2-5. Types of customer requirements.

what they are. To do this, the team makes use of market surveys, focus groups, customer interviews, and brainstorming. When trying to identify Unspokens, use all the resources and methods available.

Be patient, too. Rushing a product to market thinking you know what the customer wants is disastrous and costly. Unfulfilled unspoken requirements limit customer satisfaction; selling customers a product that falls short of expectations leaves a negative perception about the company, and it may take many years to overcome these perceptions. Take plenty of time to thoroughly learn what customers really want.

Unspokens usually fall into one of three groups:

- *Didn't remember to tell you.* In many cases, customers simply forget to say everything they want. This may occur with requests for proposal. When a client creates lengthy documents, important details often are forgotten, poorly defined, or omitted. This is often due to time or personnel constraints and an urgency to get the document out.
- *Didn't want to tell you.* There are times when customers simply do not want to give details about their requirements. For instance, these details may reveal information about them they do not want a company to have. Some customers use emotional games to test a sales staff's ability to uncover what they really want. For example, because of previous bad experiences, some people dislike buying a new car. As a result, they often withhold certain information and make the salesperson work to uncover what they really want.
- *Didn't know what it was.* Some people refer to this type of Unspoken as "I'll know it when I see it!" In many cases, customers do not tell what they want because they may not verbalize well or may think their wants foolish. To avoid embarrassment, they withhold certain information.

4. *Exciters.* Unexpected features of a product or service are Exciters. These features make the product unique and distinguish it from the competition. The features may be easy or inexpensive to provide; they may be experiments, new technologies, or simply guesses about what the customers want. They often begin as unique features that later become industry standards. In some cases, it may be possible to charge a premium for them.

An example of a successful Exciter is the cupholder Japanese manufacturers started installing in their cars in the early 1980s. Years later, U.S. automakers asked their customers what features they would like in a new car. Cupholders rose to the top of the list. U.S. automakers responded, and today cupholders are standard equipment in most U.S. and foreign-made automobiles.

FULFILLING CUSTOMER REQUIREMENTS

Customer satisfaction increases as a product or service fulfills successive customer requirement levels. Expecters are the minimal level while Exciters are the less tangible and more difficult to achieve. Nevertheless, there is a mandatory sequence to be followed when trying to achieve optimum customer satisfaction. Figure 2-6 shows the relationship between customer satisfaction and successive levels of customer requirements. Each

Figure 2-6.   QFD customer satisfaction.

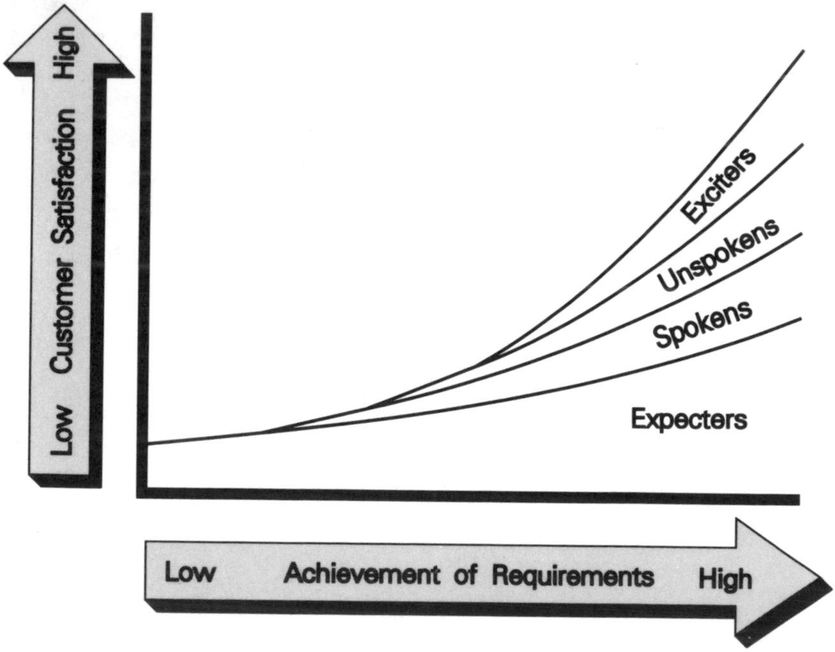

subsequent level can be achieved only after the previous one has been met.

Expecters must be satisfied first because they are the basic qualities a product must have. They serve as the buyer's first-level filter. If you do not satisfy these basic requirements, you lose the deal. In sales, when something is powerful enough to cancel a deal, it is called a "deal-buster." Well, an unfulfilled Expecter is a deal-buster! Your customer will go to a competitor who can satisfy his or her requirements.

For example, suppose a customer is thinking about buying one of your computer systems for her business. She assumes your system meets Underwriters Laboratory (UL) listings, is dependable, and uses state-of-the-art technology. These basic features are her Expecters. If they are not in your product, she probably won't buy the system from you.

Spokens increase customer satisfaction to a higher level because they go beyond product or service basics and satisfy *specific* customer requirements. For example, say your customer wants a computer system with DOS and a mouse included at no extra charge. When you include both of these features with your product, you meet her spoken requirements. Assuming your computer system meets standard functional and safety requirements, DOS and the mouse raise her level of satisfaction with your product and result in a possible sale.

Unspokens are the elusive items customers aren't aware of but want. For the computer system you sell, an unspoken may be a 124-key expanded keyboard with function keys across the top and along the left side. You've added these features to accommodate customers used to the function keys in both places. While your customer didn't specifically request these features, she is pleased the product has them and is sure this is the system she wants to buy.

Many computer systems come with a one-year warranty. To show confidence in your system, you back it with a two-year warranty. You also provide one of several popular software packages free. These product features are *Exciters* for your customer. No other vendor offers them, and they make your product unique. All your customer's requirements have been met, plus you've added two features that your competitors do not offer. Your customer sees your product as one that highly satisfies her needs. Not only will you get a sale, you will probably see other vendors adding free software and extending their warranties.

CONTINUOUS PRODUCT IMPROVEMENT

Assuming your computer system performs as stated, you should have a long-term, satisfied customer. You have earned the customer and now you must keep her. During the course of the next several years, you must support and back that customer as you promised. When it comes time to purchase again, you should be the first supplier she contacts.

In short, your quest for satisfied customers is never over. As technology, regulations, personal expectations, and product or service features change, so do your customers' requirements. For a company to remain viable, it must continually reevaluate its customer satisfaction levels. It must stay abreast of current product or service requirements. It must continually strive to hear the voice of its customers.

Once your Exciters are successful, competitors will copy them. Once consumers become used to these Exciters, these features move down in level of customer requirement to be Spokens or Expecters. In short, today's Exciters become tomorrow's Expecters, and the search for new Exciters goes on.

NOTE

1. John R. Hauser and Don Clausing. "The House of Quality," *Harvard Business Review*, May–June 1988, p. 63.

3

The Objective Statement

The QFD methodology begins with the Objective Statement. The Objective Statement, which is usually in question form, defines what you are trying to accomplish. It keeps the team focused on specific customer requirements by delineating the scope of each QFD effort so that teams undertake a single, manageable task. See Figure 3-1 for placement of the Objective Statement in the QFD system.

Developing an Objective Statement takes time, often several hours, and frequently requires a major paradigm shift. Management sometimes thinks that it knows what the customer wants and how to develop a product or service, and thus taking the time to develop an Objective Statement is seen as distracting. Managers want to develop the statement quickly and get back to their job. But teams must spend as much time as needed to develop the Objective Statement. Indeed, the first step in the QFD process is getting everyone to agree on the objective. Nothing can be accomplished until this task has been completed. And that agreement comes only from a focused Objective Statement.

For example, suppose your company, a bicycle manufacturer, decides to create a new model of bike. Before you can start designing the bike, you need to find out from customers what qualities are important to them. Therefore, your QFD team creates the following Objective Statement:

What are the important qualities of a bicycle?

If you ask consumers this question, you will get a variety of answers because the Objective Statement is too general.

Figure 3-1.   Objective within the QFD model.

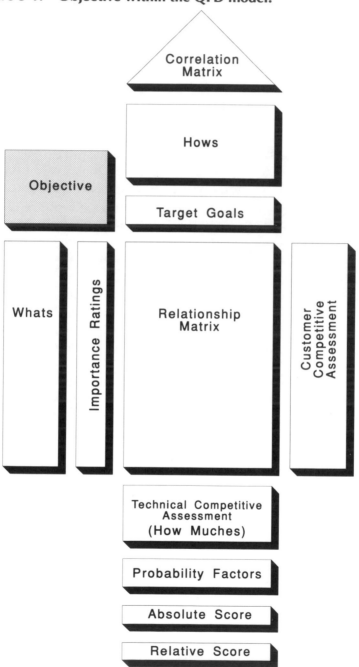

Each person bases his or her answer on personal use of a product or service. If you are going to build a mountain bicycle, then your focus group would include people who use an off-road bicycle, and they have different requirements from people who use a bike for commuting to work. Therefore, you must make sure the Objective Statement is specific to the qualities you need to identify. For a new line of off-road bicycles, a more specific Objective Statement is:

> What are the important qualities of a mountain bicycle?

This statement gives the QFD team focus. Everyone understands the intended environment in which the new bike must function. Now, the focus group of mountain bicycle riders will give you the qualities they want in a mountain bicycle.

In the bicycle example, customers did not help create the Objective Statement. However, when the product or service has been targeted to a single specific market and you wish to expand to new markets, have customers participate. Otherwise, bring the customers in *after* the team has established the Objective Statement.

For example, a paper towel manufacturer sells its product by promoting its ability to pick up spills. To expand into other potential markets, the company asked customers how they use the product. Apparently taming spills accounted for less than 25 percent of usage. Because of its thickness, the towels were used by home mechanics for cleaning their hands. As a result, the team created a new Objective Statement:

> What are the important qualities of a good shop towel?

The customers have told how they use the product. The team has an Objective Statement that focuses on a new customer need. Next, the team will ask customers what qualities they want in a shop towel.

In addition to new product development, QFD can be used to address strategic business issues, as we discussed in Chapter

1. For example, our first use of QFD had little to do with new product or service requirements. We were hired to help benchmark companies—compare their performance to a known standard. An important element of this measurement is leadership. The Objective Statement to determine the qualities of a good leader was as follows:

> What are the qualities of good leadership?

The results were used to hire dynamic new executives, develop management training programs, and establish performance criteria. Through the QFD process, we helped these companies create long-term business strategies and identify the kind of people they needed to carry them out.

DEVELOPING THE OBJECTIVE STATEMENT

When creating the Objective Statement, you must first identify how it is going to be used. If the Objective Statement is addressing customer issues, then identify the product and customer (i.e., internal, intermediate, and external).

Product Component

To begin, clearly state what the product or service is. Be specific and make sure all members of the QFD team agree. Product or service specifications may seem easy to define because the product or service often is obvious. However, many times a team begins creating an Objective Statement only to realize that a related part of the product must be developed before they can continue.

This Objective Statement contains a clearly defined product component:

> What are the important qualities of a commercial-grade ½-inch power drill?

The team has identified the specific model of power drill it will be designing. There should be no doubt about the product's characteristics and capabilities once customer input is obtained.

Customer Component

A variation of this sample Objective Statement identifies the customer. By adding the customer to the statement, the team focuses on a particular customer group:

> What qualities of a commercial-grade ½-inch power drill are important to our external customers?

FORMAT

The Objective Statement must be in a form that every member of the team understands. We've provided a basic format here. While formats can vary, we recommend this for novice QFD users because of its high success:

> What are the important _____ of _____ ?

When in doubt about the word to insert into the first blank, *qualities* usually works well. Others are *characteristics*, *elements*, and *features*. In the second blank, insert the noun naming the product or service. Then add an adjective to make the Objective Statement specific. For example, compare the three following Objective Statements:

1. What are the important qualities of a restaurant?
2. What are the important qualities of an *Italian* restaurant?
3. What are the important qualities of a *world-renowned* Italian restaurant?

The first statement asks customers to define the qualities of a restaurant without reference to type; you may find that customers are thinking about a Denny's, or a McDonald's.

Adding the adjective *Italian* in the second statement points them directly to a restaurant serving a specific type of cuisine. The addition of a single adjective in the third statement further restricts the customers' image of the restaurant. They will now be thinking about qualities needed for a restaurant to be successful worldwide.

These examples show the importance of adjectives and of correctly defining the focus of your project. Take time creating the Objective Statement. If anyone is uncertain what the Objective Statement is saying, continue to work on it. Review and revise until the team reaches consensus.

Here are some sample Objective Statements to help you develop your own:

What are the important qualities of a rocket motor?
What are the important safety features of a self-propelled lawn mower?
What are the important elements of a software program user's manual?
What are the features of excellent customer service?
What are the important characteristics of a claims service in our auto insurance company?

POORLY DEFINED STATEMENTS

You will soon be able to identify Objective Statements that are weak or unclear or that include multiple problems. Poorly defined statements result in backtracking, adding many hours, possibly days, to the QFD process, so you will want to avoid them. Fortunately, the QFD process is somewhat self-correcting. If the Objective Statement is not clear or well-defined, your QFD team will usually discover it later in the process.

Wrong-Level Statements

Many companies have already created their Objective Statement before we begin working with them. The first thing we do is review the statement with the team. In the majority of cases, either the Objective Statement is incorrect or other issues needed to be resolved first. When QFDs must be done on issues preceding the current one, we refer to this regression as *backing up a level.*

For example, our organization works with Thiokol Corporation. Thiokol is a major producer of solid propulsion systems, ordnance and composite products for the space and defense industries, and high technology, proprietary fastening systems. The company makes the solid rocket boosters for the Space Shuttle, as well as the Navy's D-5 ICBM, which is housed and fired from U.S. nuclear submarines. When Thiokol first started using QFD, one of its engineering groups hired us to help facilitate a design session. The group's Objective Statement focused on detailed functions of a specific part of a rocket motor. However, as the team proceeded, they quickly discovered that certain other questions had to be answered first by the company's internal and external customers. The QFD focus shifted to addressing these issues; once the issues were resolved, the team resumed work on the original objective.

Multiple Objectives

It is common for teams to identify multiple tasks in the Objective Statement. When this is the case, you must address each task or separate process in a separate QFD. Recognizing these multiple tasks in the early stages of QFD will reduce overall project time. The following is a multiple-task Objective Statement:

> What are the important elements of developing and implementing a new request-for-proposal system?

Developing a new request-for-proposal system is a task in itself; implementing it is another. While you may find it possible to work with a statement like this, we recommend you break it into separate QFDs. The following shows how to split this multiple-task statement:

> What are the important elements of *developing* a new request-for-proposal system?

What are the important elements of *implementing* our new request-for-proposal system?

USING A FOCUS GROUP

You find out what your customers want by asking them. One of the more popular methods for capturing their voice is the *customer focus group*. A focus group is a representative sample of customers who would use a particular product or service.

With your tentative Objective Statement defined, invite your focus group to a QFD session. The qualities they regard as important will become the *Whats* on your QFD matrix.

Whom to Invite From Your Company

Your objective will determine whom you invite from the company to your focus group meeting. It is important to invite people who best represent the departments involved. Quite often, sales, marketing, executive leadership, engineering, and manufacturing are represented.

It is important also that the QFD team represent a cross section of company functions. This stratified representation is called a *multidisciplinary team*. Using multidisciplinary teams avoids what we refer to as *myopic groups*, which can result when a majority of people represent a single function.

People focus on their jobs. If your team is made up solely of engineers, then you will get only an engineer's viewpoint. Many good ideas will be lost, never incorporated into the product or service, and the result will be an unsatisfied customer. But using a multidisciplinary team prevents this singular viewpoint. Furthermore, a synergistic effect occurs: The amount of information you receive from a multidisciplinary team exceeds the sum you would get from individual departments.

We recommend allowing no more than five people from a single department. For example, if you were going to invite ten people from your company, invite two from sales, two from marketing, two from executive leadership, two from engineering, and two from manufacturing.

The only department that can be overrepresented at this point in the QFD process is sales and marketing. These people are usually the customer's first contact with the company and often the ones the customer feels most comfortable with. In later phases of QFD, sales and marketing people should be replaced by people from other departments, such as engineering, manufacturing, or quality.

How Many Should Attend a QFD Session?

We recommend including twelve to fifteen customers in a QFD session, with a maximum of about twenty-four. With more than twenty-four customers, it is difficult to get everyone involved and capture all the ideas. However, for more common applications of QFD, involve three to eight customers.

A common sales rule for focus groups is to never have more employees than customers. If you have invited eight customers, then allow eight or fewer employees to attend. The team facilitator is counted as from the company.

If you are not sure until the day of the session how many customers are coming, create a prioritization list for the staff, ranking those who will attend. For example, if you expect eight to ten customers, list ten employees. If all ten customers attend, then allow all ten of your staff to attend; if only seven customers show up, then quietly give your Nos. 8, 9, and 10 staff members notice not to attend.

When customers arrive, the facilitator should ask if the Objective Statement accurately reflects the product or service to be discussed. If not, then the facilitator must help the group reformulate the statement. If it does, then the group moves on to identify the *Whats* discussed in the next chapter.

4

Capturing the Voice of the Customer

Now that you have your tentative Objective Statement, and your focus group and in-house team, you are ready to begin the QFD session to capture the voice of the customer. During this time, staff members must remember that they are not the customer. Their job is to remain quiet and listen to what the customers say. They may ask for clarification, but they must not lead the questioning or influence customer answers.

WHAT IS A *WHAT?*

Satisfying customers begins with listening to requirements. The Japanese refer to their requirements as customer-desired *qualities*. In QFD, these qualities become *Whats*. Think of them as *what* the customer wants—the individual characteristics of the product, service, or problem. See Figure 4-1 for the placement of *Whats* on the QFD matrix.

Qualities may also be thought of as attributes. Qualities, attributes, and requirements are all *Whats*. Your team should use whichever word seems most appropriate. For some, it is easy to describe the qualities they are looking for in a new car. For others, describing attributes may be easier. Since QFD is a method to capture the voice of your customer, use whatever term the customer prefers.

Figure 4-1. *Whats* within the QFD model.

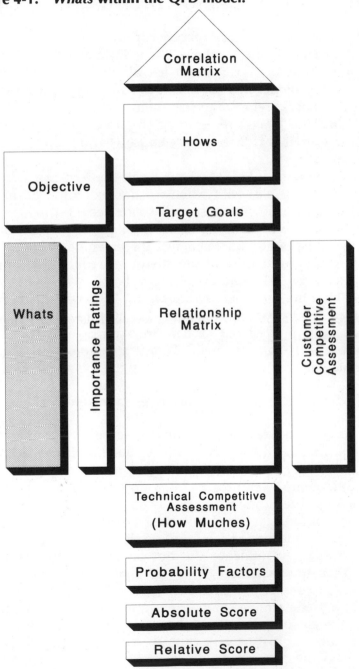

CAPTURING THE *WHATS*

There is nothing magical about capturing your customers' *Whats*; you simply ask for them. Use a dry erasable marker and a white board or flip chart to list all the requirements the customers provide. It is important to capture all of them; later you can go back, refine, and sort them.

When the *Whats* are captured, be sure each represents a single requirement. If they have more than one, break them into separate *Whats*.

How long should a *What* be? Limit them to five words or less when possible, with a ten-word maximum. Customers usually come up with descriptive phrases of three to five words. And even though you are limiting the length of the statement, be careful not to change the meaning or intent.

Capturing the voice of the customer requires skill in the art of listening. The key to getting valuable *Whats* is to write down what the customer says verbatim. When you paraphrase the statements, you risk losing the customer's true voice. Often, we translate what we hear into our own terms, and in the process change the intent. This is a common mistake. For example, let's say we ask a focus group the following question:

What are the qualities of an excellent restaurant?

When a customer responds, "One that serves something I can't make at home," then write that on your list. If the facilitator asks, "So what you are saying is you prefer a restaurant with an exotic menu?" and then writes down "exotic menu," the customer's true thought has not been captured. In this case, the customer needs to explain what he or she means before the *What* can be finalized and entered on the QFD matrix.

No one can influence the outcome of the QFD process more than the facilitator. From our experience, we recognize that an experienced facilitator in front of a novice group can lead to a predetermined outcome. For example, there are times when the customer's statement is unclear or simply too long. The facilitator must be very careful. After capturing the statement, ask the customer to shorten it. If the facilitator feels he or she must rephrase, then ask for permission to do so. Rephrasing without permission can alienate the customer, who will no longer participate. And when rephrasing, get approval of the shorter version, asking if it represents what was said. Any hesitancy by the customer should be recognized as a no— that is not what was intended. At that point, go back to the original statement and try again.

USE OF CATEGORIES

When you are listing product or service characteristics, some similarities will appear. Similar items can be grouped into categories to make the list of *Whats* more manageable. They help focus the QFD process and clarify meaning. For instance, the customer requirements for a new house fall easily into categories.

- Single-story, Southwestern design
- 2,500 livable square feet
- Four bedrooms
- Two and one-half baths
- Three-car garage
- Spacious yard

Each of these are general enough to be considered a main category. Within each of these categories, additional customer *Whats* can further define needs:

- Single-story residence
  —Southwestern style
  —Tile roof
  —Stucco exterior
  —2,500 square feet
- Four bedrooms
  —Master 300 square feet
  —Bedrooms 2 and 3 200 square feet
  —Guest or office 150 square feet

- Two and one-half baths
  —Full bath and shower in master bedroom
  —Full bath shared between two of the bedrooms
  —Half bath near the family room and kitchen
- Three-car garage
  —2-car door + 1-car door
  —Large, 100-square-foot work area
  —Walk-in closet for storage (100 square feet)

THE IMPORTANCE RATINGS

Although all of your customer's *Whats* probably are important, QFD provides a systematic method to identify which are more important than others. Importance Ratings play a key role in the QFD process. First, they serve as weighting factors. Later, these customer-assigned weights are multipliers for other numbers in the matrix, affecting certain statistical conclusions. No other part of the matrix has as much influence on the outcome of the process. Therefore, Importance Ratings must accurately reflect the customer's opinions. You may have to go to great effort and expense to satisfy high-importance requirements. Therefore, you want to be sure that the ratings accurately reflect customer needs.

Symbols and Scales

The original Japanese QFD scales used symbols representing values of 1, 3, and 9 (see Figure 4-2), familiar ones in their culture: Win, Place, and Show from the horseracing tracks. Their symbols accomplished four things:

1. They provided icons for quick reference when reviewing complex matrices.
2. They minimized influencing the participants by not having numbers present during the evaluations.
3. They were a simplified form of writing compared to their pictoral characters.

Figure 4-2. Japanese QFD symbols.

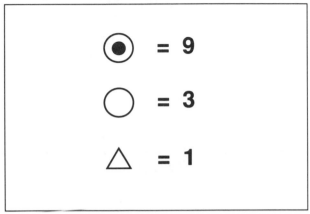

4. On rare occasions, the graphics provided a common language when QFDs were conducted with non-Japanese-speaking people.

When QFD migrated to the United States, the original intent of the Japanese symbols became less important. As teams became familiar with the symbols, they found little difference in representing values as pictures or as numerals.

Thus Importance Rating scales may vary. The Japanese sometimes use a 1-to-9 scale, other times a 1-to-5 scale. Nevertheless, on all scales, 1 represents low importance and 5 or the highest value shows high importance. In any event, only whole numbers are recommended.

We prefer a 1-to-5 scale because it makes customers more selective in assigning ratings. The smaller scale means less difference between selections, as a result it may take longer to assign weights to each item. When first establishing your ratings, begin with the 1-to-5 scale. Then, if your team wants to experiment with larger scales, do so. Most important, use the scale, and possibly symbols, that your customers and team find most meaningful.

Assigning the Ratings

The team can use one or more guidelines to help assign the Importance Ratings. These methods provide a systematic way to review the *Whats* on your list and rank them in importance.

Drivers

When *Whats* occur before other *Whats* or are more important than other *Whats*, they are called *drivers*. You always give a
driver a higher Importance Rating than those that follow it,
usually a factor of 4 or 5. You can also identify drivers in terms
of the customer requirements described in Chapter 2. Drivers
are Expecters or Spokens.

We recently helped a large aerospace company create a
supplier development program. Delivery performance was key
for measuring suppliers, so it created the following Objective
Statement.

"What are the important qualities of delivery?"

Using a multidisciplinary team with people from engineering,
manufacturing, quality, procurement, and marketing, we created a list of *Whats*. The drivers for these *Whats* were "no
inspection" and "cost and logistics." Notice in Figure 4-3 that
"no inspection" has a rating of 5, and "cost and logistics" is a
4.

Multiple Passes

Participants unfamiliar with QFD tend to give every *What*
an Importance Rating of 5. To overcome this problem we
developed a technique we call *multiple passes*. As the name
implies, the QFD facilitator takes the team through the list
several times. We have found that at least three passes are
needed to properly assign the ratings. Thus, a dozen *Whats* can
easily take a team two hours to process. Nevertheless, take the
time to make three passes before accepting your final values;
the repeated effort is worthwhile.

For instance, an aircraft manufacturer was a supplier for a
division of the armed forces. This division had prepared a
request for proposal (RFP) that was several hundred pages
long. In it were a variety of upgrades to be installed before
there would be another order for aircraft. The company was

Figure 4-3.   Important delivery qualities and their ratings.

What are the important elements of Delivery?	Import. Rating (1 to 5)
On-time	3
Quantity	3
Received condition	2
Marking	1
No inspection	5
Paperwork	2
Cost & logistics	4

anxious to better understand the requirements described in the RFP, so it began the QFD process.

As the meeting started, the QFD process got people talking face-to-face. The facilitator put aside the huge RFP, and the hundreds of pages of documentation were reduced to the following *Whats*.

- Fly higher
- Fly faster
- Carry more weight
- Be more maneuverable

Going into the process, both parties knew that the improvements were mutually exclusive. The *Whats* were given Importance Ratings using a type of multiple pass called *questioning:*

If we can only accomplish one of these items for you, which one should it be?

"Carry more weight" was found to be most important, so it was assigned an Importance Rating of 5. Next was asked:

If we find we are capable of accomplishing *an* additional item, which one should we complete?

The response was "more maneuverability," which was assigned an Importance Rating of 4.

The manufacturer asked this question two more times, assigning a progressively lower rating to items on the list. When finished, the list looked like this:

Fly higher 3
Fly faster 2
Carry more weight 5
Be more maneuverable 4

This type of questioning can help both parties quickly determine Importance Ratings for each *What*. In a very short time, the aircraft manufacturer knew where to focus the company's resources. Now, instead of doing what was easiest for the company, the manufacturer would give the armed forces specifically what it had asked for, in the order asked for.

Uniform Distribution

When the facilitator recognizes that the customer is having difficulty assigning the full range of ratings, *uniform distribution* can be of help. This situation is common to focus groups with people unaccustomed to ranking product or service requirements. As a result, their initial reaction is that *all* the requirements are important. The facilitator must reinforce that all of the *Whats* are important, and that the process simply compares one to another.

Uniform distribution means that values are spread evenly among the *Whats*. There is approximately an equal number of each value rated 1 through 5.

To determine what the uniform distribution should be, use the following method:

1. Divide the total number of *Whats* by 5 (5 is the range of scores).
2. Round off as needed.
3. Use the answer as a guide for the number of times a value is assigned a *What*.

For example, assume your list consists of ten *Whats:* 10 ÷ 5 = 2. Therefore, the team should assign approximately two 1's, two 2's, two 3's, two 4's, and two 5's.

This method points out whether the team has assigned too many high values and too few low values. Before going further, the team adjusts the ratings, since they will strongly impact the QFD results later on.

Priority Inversion

The fourth guideline for assigning ratings, priority inversion, is used mostly when QFD is a problem-solving tool. In a problem-solving situation, one key *What* represents the desired outcome, but before achieving that *What*, sometimes other *Whats* must occur first. This is a *priority inversion*.

When you recognize a priority inversion is occurring, reassign values to the entire list. What was assigned a rating of 5 will often be reassigned a lower rating; what was originally a 1 or 2 may become a 4 or 5.

For example, when the aerospace company did a multiple pass on its list of *Whats*, it discovered that what was thought of as a driver was really a *result* of other events.

As the team began flowcharting its internal processes, it discovered an interesting phenomenon. Before any of the company's systems could recognize a part, the part must carry the correct marking, or identification. "Marking" became the primary driver for the list of *Whats*.

First, the part was identified according to its markings. Then it could be referenced in the computerized system and the condition determined. The condition data determined how the product should be packaged for shipping; improperly packaged products could be rejected.

Equally important was having the supplier provide the

appropriate paperwork with each delivery. If not, the client could reject the delivery. In addition, the client was developing its suppliers to provide statistical processing control (SPC) data with their shipments. The company intended to specify the exact SPC data in each supplier's contract, recorded on the paperwork for the delivery. When deliveries arrived, receiving verified the SPC data and delivery could be made. With the quantity received compared to that ordered, the part could be identified and, its condition verified, accepted for delivery. An invoice could be forwarded to procurement and accounts payable for payment. This is what the company referred to as its cost and logistics.

Thus, if all other criteria were satisfied, "inspection" could be the least important item on the list. The team therefore reassigned the Importance Ratings. Figure 4-4 shows the list of *Whats* and the Importance Ratings before and after the priority inversion.

INTERPRETING THE IMPORTANCE RATINGS

It is imperative that all *Whats* rated 5 be considered for your new product or service. These are your customer's Expecters

Figure 4-4.   Effect of priority inversion.

Before		After	
What are the Important elements of Delivery?	**Import. Rating** (1 to 5)	**What are the Important elements of Delivery?**	**Import. Rating** (1 to 5)
On-time	3	On-time	3
Quantity	3	Quantity	3
Received condition	2	Received condition	4
Marking	1	Marking	5
No inspection	5	No inspection	1
Paperwork	2	Paperwork	4
Cost & logistics	4	Cost & logistics	2

Figure 4-5. New home requirements.

(I.R. = Importance Ratings: 1 = low, 5 = high)

Category	What	I.R.
Single-story residence	S/W style with tile roof	4
	Stucco exterior	2
	2,500 square feet	5
Four bedrooms	Master bdrm = 300 sq ft	5
	Bdrms 2 & 3 = 200 sq ft	4
	Guest/office = 150 sq ft	2
Two & one-half baths	Full bath & shower in master	5
	Bath shared between bedrooms	3
	1/2 bath near family room/kitchen	4
Three-car garage	2 car door + 1 car door	4
	Large 100 sq ft work area	4
	100 sq ft walk-in storage closet	3

and Spokens! Customers will be satisfied only when these requirements are met. It may be more challenging to satisfy 5-rated items than lower ones. They may stretch your resources and extend your capabilities to the limit. Nevertheless, satisfying these *Whats* is critical. Fulfilling requirements of lower importance will have little effect on customer satisfaction. Figure 4-5 uses the new home criteria mentioned earlier in the chapter to show Importance Ratings in the QFD matrix.

5

The Customer Competitive Assessment

The *Whats* list has captured the voice of the customer. You have well-defined customer perceptions of a quality product or service. Now you are ready to use these perceptions as the basis for a comparison between you and your competitors. The Customer Competitive Assessment verifies that the customer requirements developed by the focus group are indeed what is perceived as important by the larger customer population. (Note: In QFD, there are two types of competitive assessments. The Customer Competitive Assessment measures customer perception of the product or service relative to the competition. The other is the Technical Competitive Assessment, used to establish technical specifications for your product or service; the latter is covered in Chapter 7.) See Figure 5-1 for the placement of Customer Competitive Assessment on the QFD matrix.

The Customer Competitive Assessment uses data collected from customers as the basis for comparison. These data are depicted graphically to show how well your competition meets the *Whats* established by your focus group. It is a highly effective method to identify gaps and conflicts, or to determine competitive position. As you will see, you can use single or multiple graphs to show customer ratings and competitive performance.

The Customer Competitive Assessment will enable you to:

1. Verify that your list of product or service requirements

Figure 5-1. Customer Competitive Assessment within the QFD model.

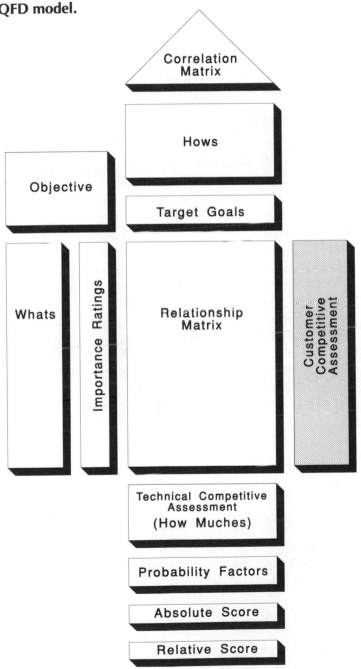

are ones that are important to your customer population.
2. Capture additional customer requirements. These new
requirements could be Unspokens or Exciters.
3. Identify how customers perceive your target product in
comparison to your competitors'. Discover the
strengths and weaknesses of your product or service.
4. Identify weaknesses in your competitors' products,
which can be opportunities for you.

Cautions: The Customer Competitive Assessment provides
quantitative data to help you determine if your product or
service will sell. This information will allow you to make
informed business decisions, but your success depends heavily
on the data you gather during this portion of the process.
Unfortunately, marketing data take time to collect, and the
Customer Competitive Assessment takes time to work. While
the other portions of QFD often can be completed in a few
days, collecting marketing data may take months. Many organizations want quick results and do not take the time to do this
necessary market research and analysis. Taking shortcuts or
omitting this step reduces the reliability of information on
which to base your business decisions. If your competitors use
the data and you don't, they possess a power you do not have.
So take the time now to validate your *Whats* findings and back
up hunches with statistics.

HOW TO USE THE CUSTOMER
COMPETITIVE ASSESSMENT

To verify the *Whats* established by your initial focus group, you
can use another research method or a combination of methods,
such as additional focus groups, customer interviews, existing
market survey data, or any other form of market research
available. If you select additional focus groups, they must again
be representative of the customer population. The additional
focus groups could come from regional offices of your customers instead of local offices, or they could be customers not

invited to the earlier sessions. Group size should be from five to ten, and participants should represent the same perspective relative to the product or service under study.

When using a combination of data, compare focus group ratings of *Whats* with survey results. When ratings are dissimilar, ask each focus group for the reasons for a rating. This information could identify a poorly stated question on the survey and could raise or lower the rating given a *What* in the Competitive Assessment.

Next your team members identify which competitors you will use for comparison. They select competitors who are successfully offering a similar product or service, or whose name customers mention. When using a survey to compare your product with a competitor's, your list of *Whats* is the basis for your questions and you use the same scale to rate your competitor's product or service as yours. The scale used for the survey and by focus groups should be the same one used for Importance Ratings.

When constructing your survey, use open-ended questions to make sure it captures any other *Whats* that are important to the customer. Do this by asking them what other requirements are important. Also ask customers to name the company that satisfies a requirement best. For example, "Who does this best: Company A, B, C, or D?" The results of this question tell your team who is considered the "Best in Class" for satisfying this requirement, and you can use this information as a target for your performance.

Lastly, avoid using engineers or technical staff to perform the Customer Competitive Assessment. Their technical knowledge can narrow and restrict customers' statements.

ANALYZING THE ASSESSMENT

Figure 5-2 is a simple Customer Competitive Assessment. A survey was developed and customers were asked to rate each *What* on a scale of 1 to 5. The average score for each *What* is listed in the column called Survey Score. After the survey scores were entered, a line graph was created. The graph is a

Figure 5-2. Typical Customer Competitive Assessment.

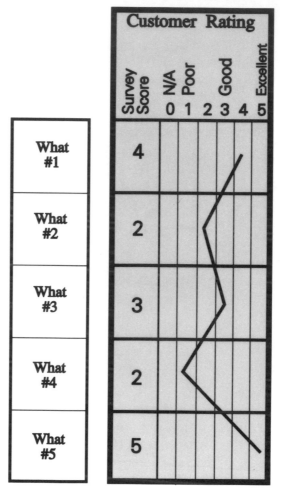

visual representation of the *Whats* ratings, showing how survey respondents weighted the requirements developed by the focus group. In this instance, survey respondents said that *What* 1 was a good feature, and rated it a 4.

In addition, the surveys are studied for new requirements added by respondents. These requirements are added to the list of *Whats* and presented to future focus groups for their reaction. Should focus groups agree that these new requirements are important, they will be added to the list of *Whats*

Figure 5-3. Customer Competitive Assessment with company analysis.

	Competitive Company Analysis				Rating						
	Company				Highest Score	N/A 0	Poor 1	2	Good 3	4	Excellent 5
	A	B	C	D							
What #1	2	1	2	4	4						
What #2	1	1	2	1	2						
What #3	3	3	2	1	3						
What #4	1	1	2	2	2						
What #5	5	4	4	5	5						

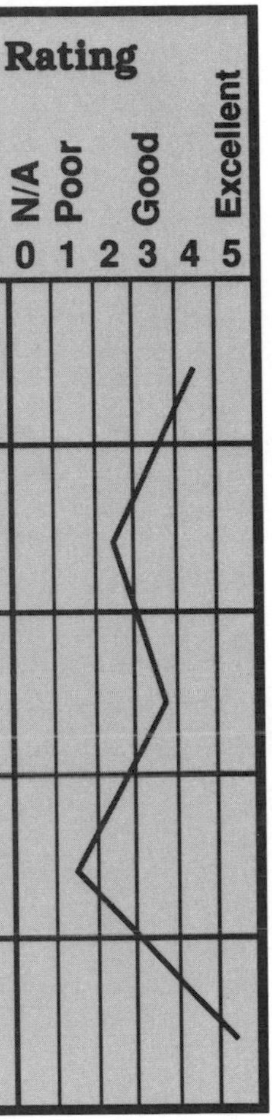

and the Importance Ratings will be reassigned according to focus group decisions.

Ratings for competitive companies were asked on the survey, and Figure 5-3 shows those competitive results displayed in a table and graphic format. In this example, four competitive companies were evaluated as to how well each's product satisfied each *What*. The scores represent survey and later focus group data indicating customer perceptions. For example, company A was rated 2 for *What* 1, indicating low customer satisfaction. For the same *What*, company D was rated 4, meaning customers perceived this company as fulfilling the requirement quite well.

The highest score for each *What* was carried to the line graph, since the company decided to use the highest scoring competitor as its minimum performance standard. (These performance levels are used again in the Technical Competitive Assessment because they are the minimum performance acceptable to the customer.)

With the Customer Competitive Assessment complete, the team has a clear idea of what product or service requirements will satisfy the customer. Using this information, the team may reevaluate its Importance Ratings, and may add new customer requirements to its existing list of *Whats*. The team now decides to either accept or retest this new set of requirements.

6

The *Hows* to Achieve Your Customer's Requirements

Up to this point, our focus was on identifying the problem. Now we move to solving the problem. The team learns how to go about meeting the customer's requirements as it enters the analysis and problem-solving portion of QFD.

A MULTIDISCIPLINARY APPROACH

Hows are ways of achieving *Whats*. Virtually any idea that can help solve a problem is a *How*. *Hows* consist of processes, facilities, and methods. They also are people, departments, and functions in the organization. See Figure 6-1 for the placement of *Hows* on the QFD matrix.

This part of the QFD process uses the collective knowledge of your company. It is extremely important to be multidisciplinary at this point. Solving problems requires different ideas and differing perspectives; no single person in a company has sufficient knowledge to resolve all the issues. QFD helps you use your company's collective knowledge in an organized and methodical way.

The team should include representatives of all the functions in your organization. Avoid having more than half the team from a single function or department. For instance, if you include fifteen engineers, then also include fifteen nonengineers.

If you are using QFD to determine how to design a new

Figure 6-1.   *Hows* **within the QFD model.**

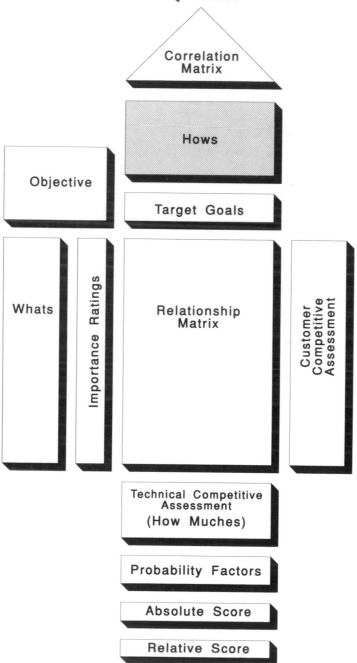

product, only half of the team should be design engineers. Make sure departments such as accounting, sales, finance, quality, procurement, and manufacturing are included. Because of the particular knowledge and experience an individual has with certain aspects of the business, he or she can dramatically change the team's thought process. This is a *positive* aspect of the multidisciplinary team approach. Encourage it, and better solutions will be a natural occurrence.

COLLECTING THE *HOWS*

The process starts with "blue sky" thinking. The facilitator holds a brainstorming session for ways to achieve the customer requirements. This is an opportunity for everyone to offer possible solutions to the *Whats*. None of the ideas should be evaluated at this point. Just capture them, so that later in the process the team can evaluate each in detail.

For example, assume your company is designing a new computer for the aerospace industry. The team has identified the power supply as a critical component. Here are some *Hows* that might have been generated during the brainstorming session.

1. Use an existing design.
2. Modify an existing design.
3. Develop a new design.
4. Purchase a complete assembly from a supplier.

Limit the brainstorming sessions to about four hours. Depending on the size of your *Whats* list, several sessions may be required. The process normally moves quickly.

Start developing the *Hows* by asking the team members for their ideas. Use the following question:

What are some of the ways we can help accomplish the list of *Whats?*

Write the ideas on a flip chart or white board. Capture all that are offered.

There is no limit to the number of *Hows* you can have. A rule of thumb is to expect at least twice the number of *Whats*; if your *Whats* list is eight items long, expect to develop approximately sixteen *Hows*. One interesting phenomenon is that, when the *Whats* list is five to eight items long, the average number of *Hows* is thirteen. But there are no specific rules for the number of *Hows*; therefore, do not limit the creativity of your team. (As the number of *Hows* approaches twenty-four, however, the list becomes less manageable for the Relationship Matrix that comes later in the process. If necessary, you'll have to break the matrix analysis task into several meetings.)

How Do You Know When You Have All the Hows?

When your team cannot suggest anymore *Hows*, bring the session to a close. If you need to add more *Hows* later, you can do so. Sometimes people come up with more *Hows* after they evaluate the list in subsequent steps. The QFD process allows later additions.

When we feel the team has provided all possible *Hows*, we formally announce that the process is concluded and we will move on to the next portion of QFD. This helps team members make the mental switch to the next phase. Also, this is the time to acknowledge how much progress has been made and how much the team has accomplished.

THE TARGET GOALS

Once you have a list of potential *Hows*, you need to identify the best ones. As with *Whats*, *Hows* must be quantified, or else it will be difficult to know if they have been accomplished. Target Goals are a preliminary filter to help determine if a *How* is quantifiable. They indicate if the *How* can increase something, decrease something, or achieve a specific goal.

Suppose your customers tell you they want a quieter ride in a vehicle. A suggested *How* may be that an improved exhaust system will help quiet engine noise. Thus, the Target Goal for the improved exhaust system would be to *decrease* noise. If customers tell you they want better performance, then a suggested *How* may be to provide a more powerful engine. The Target Goal is to *increase* the power of the engine. If customers tell you they want the vehicle to achieve a minimum of 30 miles per gallon, then the corresponding *How* is to design a new engine and the Target Goal is to *achieve* 30 miles per gallon.

Target Goals are located between the *Hows* and the Relationship Matrix in the QFD model (see Figure 6-2). Three symbols are used to represent Target Goals: the up arrow to show an increase, the down arrow to show decrease, and the bull's-eye to show target value, which is assigned in the *How Muches* (see Figure 6-3).

The facilitator asks the team to assign a Target Goal to each of the *Hows* and mark it with one of the three symbols. Any *How* difficult to assign a symbol to should be reassessed. If a Target Goal cannot be assigned, *then eliminate the* How *from the list!* It is not a measurable solution. Figure 6-4 shows how Target Goals have been assigned to a list of *Hows*.

THE CORRELATION MATRIX— AKA THE "ROOF"

The Correlation Matrix, or "Roof," is shown in Figure 6-5. The Correlation Matrix takes the shape of a pitched roof because it is actually an *XY* grid that has been rotated 45 degrees. It shows positive and negative relationships among the *Hows*. That is, it is used to determine which *Hows* support one another and where conflicts can occur. The Roof also indicates where additional research and development efforts may be needed. Using the Roof can help you spot a resource that can be used for multiple purposes. This is extremely valuable because these relationships are rarely identified or documented elsewhere.

To illustrate its use, consider a hydraulic pump manufacturer that was recently asked to supply a customer with a different type of pump. It appeared that the customer's requirements would call for a totally new design. Sales was eager to close the deal, but engineering wanted to use QFD to

Figure 6-2.   Target Goals within the QFD model.

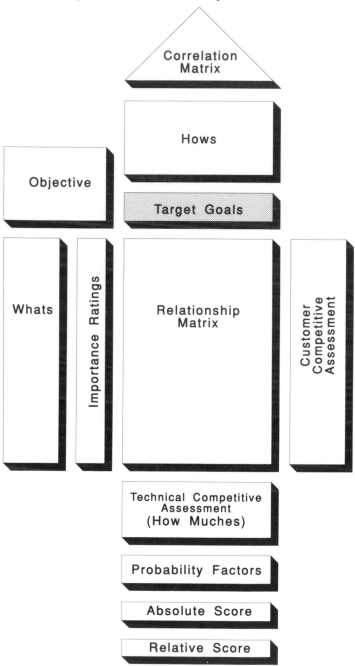

Figure 6-3. Target Goal symbols.

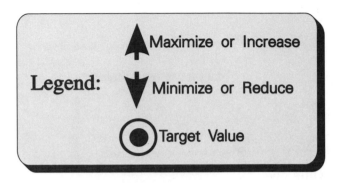

Figure 6-4. Target Goals assigned to matrix.

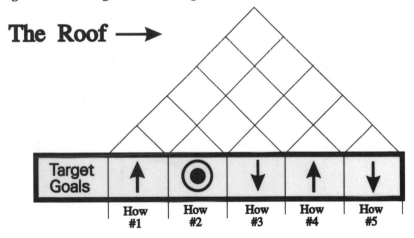

determine the impact of the new design on that department and on the entire organization.

As the company worked through the QFD process, the Correlation Matrix uncovered a conflict. The company did not have the technical resources to develop another new product while continuing development of its existing product. But the Roof also showed that the company could combine its engi-

Figure 6-5.   Correlation Matrix within the QFD model.

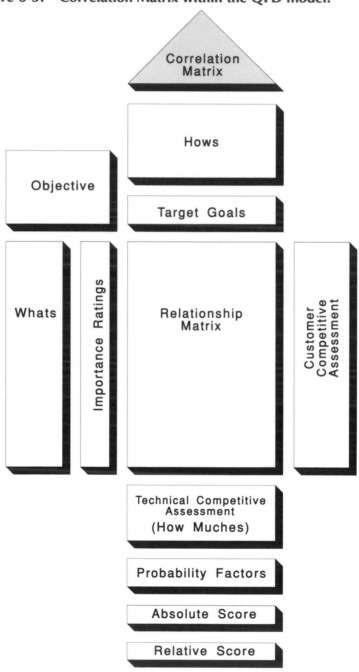

neering efforts and develop both pumps concurrently. Since the designs were somewhat similar, many features of the new pump could be incorporated into the existing product.

Had it not used the Correlation Matrix, the company would have worked on both pumps simultaneously, not realizing that they had common features that required the same engineering. There would have been two engineering teams developing pumps with similar parts, and manufacturing would have made many more parts than necessary.

It would have taken two to three months for the effects of this decision to surface. Schedules would have started slipping, and overtime or additional help would have been required. Delivery would have been late for both pumps. Schedule slippages and cost overruns would have resulted in cost cutting throughout the engineering and manufacturing processes. Both products would have suffered from less than optimum quality and poor customer satisfaction.

Company officials said that the Correlation Matrix enabled them to get the customer's business and save considerable costs. This is the value of the matrix, let's move on to how it works.

Symbols

Four symbols are used in the Correlation Matrix: a strong positive relationship, represented by two plus signs; a positive relationship, represented by one plus sign; a negative relationship, represented by one negative sign; and a strong negative relationship, represented by two negatives turned sideways. (Typically, two *x*s are used for the strong negative relationship to eliminate confusion.) These symbols are shown in Figure 6-6. The positive symbols show which *Hows* support each other. The negative symbols show which *Hows* are in conflict and where tradeoffs may be required. As in the previous example where certain *Hows* supported one another. Similar engineering efforts could be combined and a new pump could be developed concurrent with development on an existing pump.

When all the *Hows* are entered on the QFD matrix and the Target Goals assigned, you are ready to assign the relationship

Figure 6-6.   Correlation Matrix symbols.

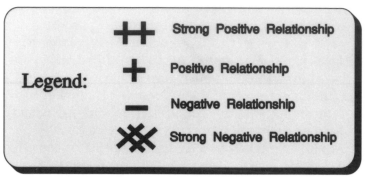

symbols. Figure 6-7 shows the matrix and how symbols are assigned. Starting with *How* 1, ask if there is a relationship between *How* 1 and *How* 2. If there is a positive relationship, then enter a plus (+) in the box where the two intersect. Continue with *How* 1, moving up the column toward the peak to the second box, and ask if there is a relationship between *How* 1 and *How* 3. In our example, there is no relationship, therefore no symbol is placed in the box.

Continue with *How* 1 to the third box, and ask if there is a relationship between *How* 1 and *How* 4. In our example, there is a strong negative relationship; therefore, the ✕ symbol is placed in the box. Continue with *How* 1 until all relationships between it and the other *Hows* have been tested.

Now test for relationships between *How* 2 and the remaining *Hows*. In our example, there is a negative relationship between *How* 2 and *How* 3. Note that the negative (−) symbol is placed in the box at the intersection. At first it may be difficult to identify the appropriate column above *How* 2, however, with a little practice your eye will become familiar with these leaning columns and how they intersect. Continue testing for relationships for all other *Hows*. This way of proceeding prevents you from becoming confused about which *Hows* you have tested and repeating any. Figure 6-8 shows the proper sequence.

Figure 6-7. Using the Correlation Matrix to determine interrelationships among *Hows*.

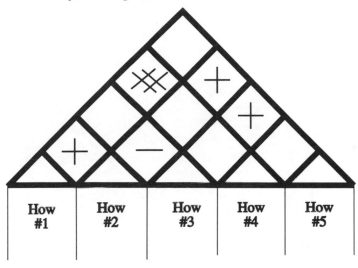

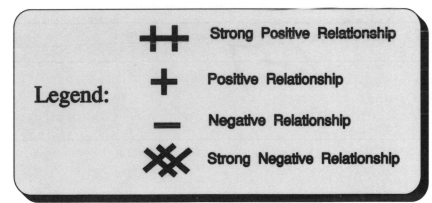

Analysis of Results

A positive relationship indicates that two *Hows* may have *synergy*, while a negative relationship indicates that two *Hows* may have an *adverse* effect on each other. When negative correlations occur, one or more tradeoffs may be necessary. But don't resort to a tradeoff immediately; try to find other solutions. For example, a negative correlation may exist because your organization does not have a particular process to make a part.

Figure 6-8.   Sequence for working through the Correlation Matrix.

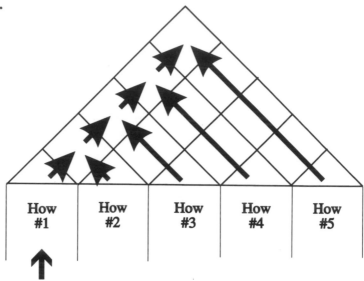

A. Starting with the first *How*, enter the Correlation Symbol indicating the relationship to each of the other *Hows*.

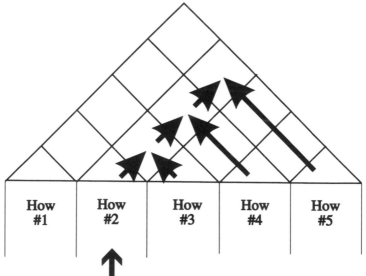

B. Move to the second *How* and enter the Correlation Symbol indicating the relationship to each of the remaining *Hows*.

However, investments in research to develop that process could provide a solution and result in a competitive advantage. Experience shows that many optimal product designs and production processes have been the result of tradeoffs.

Some tradeoffs require high-level decisions because they involve more than one department or function. If a team needs to know whether to proceed with development of a new process, that decision should come immediately from upper management. As a rule, issues identified in the matrix should be resolved quickly to reduce overall QFD process time. (Note: Negative correlations also can be resolved by adjusting the values of the *How Muches*, explained in Chapter 7.) When a tradeoff must be made, make it in favor of the customer. Do not make tradeoffs according to what's easiest for the company.

When no negative correlations exist, reevaluate the matrix. You may be doing something wrong.

7

Technical Assessment and Difficulty Analysis

There are two parts to technical assessment—the Technical Competitive Assessment, similar to the Customer Competitive Assessment but involving technical details of the product or service, and the Objective Values, or *How Muches*, whereby engineering specifications are established. Whereas in the Customer Competitive Assessment customers provide the data for the assessment, in the Technical Competitive Assessment engineers and technical people provide the assessment data. See Figure 7-1 for where Technical Assessment belongs in the QFD model.

THE TECHNICAL COMPETITIVE ASSESSMENT

To compare the competition's technical standards to your own, you use the same competitors and products as for the Customer Competitive Assessment described in Chapter 5. However, this time you compare *Hows* instead of *Whats*.

Expanding on the example we used in Chapter 6, the *What* used was a "quieter ride," and the *How* developed was an "improved exhaust system." Whereas the Customer Competitive Assessment compared the quietness of one car to another, the Technical Competitive Assessment compares each car's sound level in decibels.

We recommend comparing two or three competitors' prod-

Figure 7-1. Technical Assessment within the QFD model.

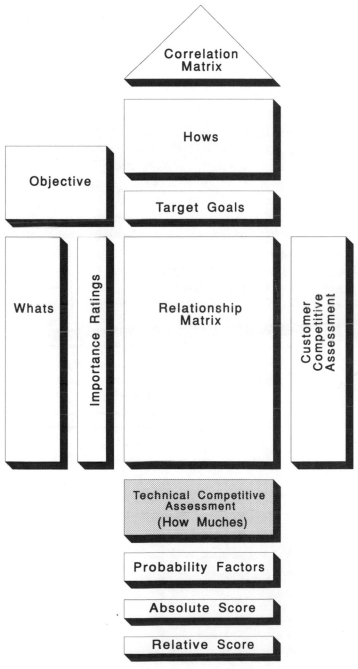

ucts, your current product, and your target product. Enter each product as a separate row on the matrix. In keeping with the other numeric conventions in the QFD process, use the standard 1-to-5 scale, where 1 equals low performance and 5 equals high. For each *How*, enter a value that indicates the level of competitor performance, your current product's performance, and your target product's performance. The result is an indication of how your current product fares—below, equivalent, or surpassing your competitor's product. You will also see if improvements are needed in your target product.

For example, the team, which includes engineers and technical people at this point, does a Technical Competitive Assessment rating two or three of their competitors' cars, their current car, and the target car. The ratings may be based on research data or best guesses. Team members reach consensus on a score for each *How* and each competitor. Then their scores are displayed either in a table format (like that created for the Customer Competitive Assessment) or on a graph. In Figure 7-2 we've graphed the highest score given one of the competi-

Figure 7-2. Technical Competitive Assessment.

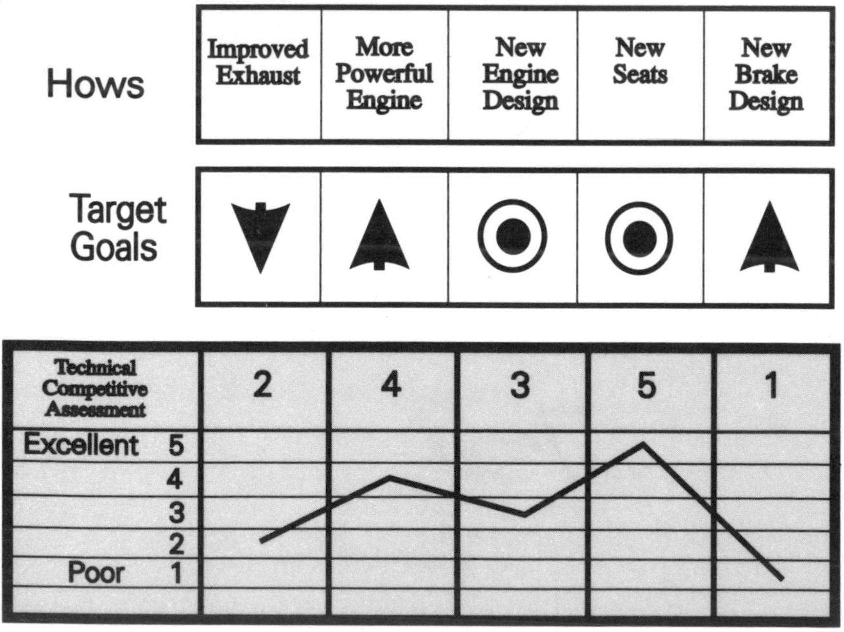

tors. Later when the team sets Objective Values for each *How*, they will refer to the highest-scoring competitor's technical specifications and set the Objective Values to either meet or surpass them.

OBJECTIVE VALUES

Objective Values are the engineering specifications your team establishes for the product or service. The team determines *how much* you must do to be competitive in the marketplace and to what extent each *How* must be changed. For that reason, Objective Values are often referred to as *How Muches*. While Target Goals are indicators for changing the general direction of a *How*, Objective Values are quantifiable measurements for each *How*. You create Objective Values according to industry and company standards. Evaluate what your customer wants and what the competition offers, then decide on the standard. Enter the measurement as the *How Much* for each *How*.

When you cannot make a comparison of products owing to lack of information, your marketing and technical staff need to further research the industry. When it is impossible to quantitatively assess the competition, make realistic guesses or assume your competition is doing as well as you are. When doing your research, you may discover a void in the market, in which case you will have identified an opportunity to establish a new standard and product Exciter while filling a market niche.

Let's expand on the example we introduced in Chapter 6. We determined that customers want a quieter ride in a vehicle, and the team specified an improved exhaust system as the *How* to achieve this. The Target Goal for the improved exhaust is a down arrow, indicating a decrease is needed. In the Technical Competitive Assessment, you find a competitor's exhaust system has a sound level of 68 decibels. Therefore, your *How Much* is "a sound level lower than 68 decibels."

For the *What* "better performance," the specific *How* was a "more powerful engine." The Target Goal is an up arrow, indicating an increase in engine power is needed. The Technical Competitive Assessment reveals that competitor performance is "0 to 60 in 13.5 seconds." So you define your *How Much* as "0 to 60 in less than 12 seconds" or a 25 percent increase in horsepower (HP).

For a third customer requirement of a vehicle capable of getting a minimum of 30 miles per gallon, the *How* is to "design a new engine," the Target Goal is a bull's-eye, and the *How Much* is "30 miles per gallon." Your competitor's performance is 27 miles per gallon. Figure 7-3 illustrates the placement of these *How Muches* in the Technical Assessment Matrix.

The Price of Admission

When you are designing a new product or modifying an existing one, the *How Muches* define how well your product must perform to satisfy potential customers. The Objective Values become your minimum standards for entering the marketplace. If you cannot achieve these standards, then the QFD

Figure 7-3.   Objective Values.

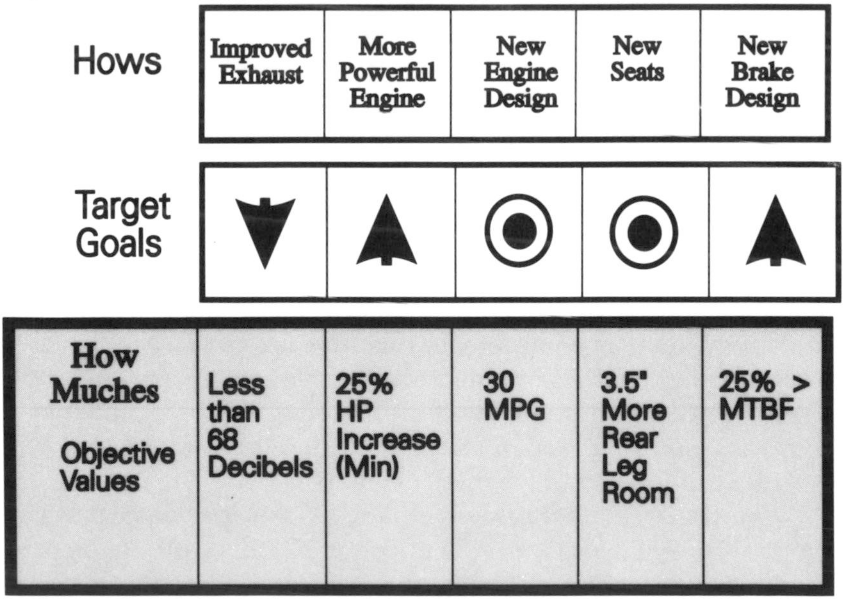

Hows	Improved Exhaust	More Powerful Engine	New Engine Design	New Seats	New Brake Design
Target Goals	▼	▲	◉	◉	▲
How Muches **Objective Values**	Less than 68 Decibels	25% HP Increase (Min)	30 MPG	3.5" More Rear Leg Room	25% > MTBF

process has already served you well. It has told you not to bother entering the market; your product will not be as good as your competitors'. For this reason, the *How Muches* are also referred to as the Price of Admission.

Using the same example, if your new vehicle is not quieter than 70 decibels, does not accelerate to 60 miles per hour in 12 seconds, and does not get 30 miles to a gallon, you will not satisfy customer requirements. Achieving all these requirements may take ten or more years. However, if you can improve on what the competition offers, then it may be worth the effort and expense to develop a vehicle meeting these requirements.

DIFFICULTY AND PROBABILITY

The Difficulty Analysis in the QFD method allows you to factor in your perceived probability of achieving a specific *How*. Once you have done the Technical Competitive Analysis and determined your Objective Values, the team is in a position to consider the probability of success.

The Probability Factor is a weight assigned to each *How* and affects the final QFD results. For instance, a low Probability Factor can indicate that a current solution is not going to be competitive. It can also indicate that new technology, systems, or methods must be adopted or developed.

In keeping with the other numeric conventions in the QFD process, the standard 1-to-5 scale is used for the Probability Factors: 1 = low probability, 5 = high.

When we train companies to use QFD, we use Probability Factors rather than Difficulty Factors, which are part of the Japanese version of QFD. The logic underlying Difficulty Factors is confusing to many people. The Japanese give low values to difficult goals and high values to easy ones—the reverse of scoring used in the rest of the QFD process. Later, they multiply this number by its Absolute Score and end up with the same results as we do using Probability Factors. See Figure 7-4 for a comparison of the two methods.

Since many organizations had difficultly with the Japanese

Figure 7-4. Comparison of matrices using Difficulty and Probability Factors.

A. Difficulty Factor

Objective Statement	How A	How B	How C
Absolute Score	10	9	8
Difficulty Factor	x 3	x 4	x 5
Conclusion:	30	36	40

B. Probability Factor

Objective Statement	How A	How B	How C
Absolute Score	10	9	8
Probability Factor	x 3	x 4	x 5
Conclusion:	30	36	40

method, we reversed the scale and changed the name of the factors.

To determine the Probability Factor for a *How*, ask:

What is the probability of accomplishing this *How*?

Figure 7-5.   Probability Factors within the QFD model.

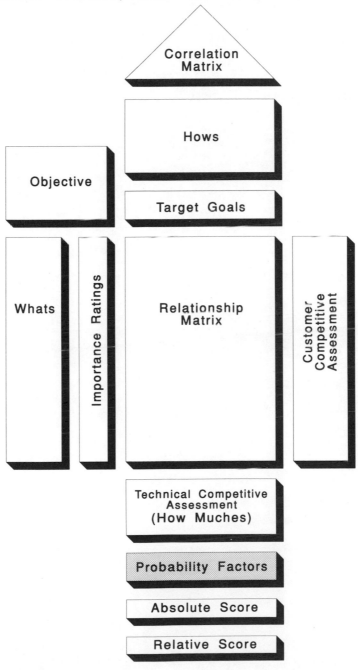

Assign a 5 if there is a high probability of achieving it and a 1 if there is a low probability. Use the full range (1 to 5) of values when assigning Probability Factors; these are later multiplied by the Absolute Score for each *How*. Probability Factors are placed on the QFD model beneath the Technical Competitive Assessment (see Figure 7-5). Their relationship to Absolute and Relative Scores is discussed further in Chapter 8.

8

The Relationship Matrix

By now, you have decided what new market you want to enter (Objective Statement), you've listened to what your customers want (captured the voice of the customer *Whats*), compared your products or services with your competitors' (Customer Competitive Assessment), identified how you are going to achieve the customers' requirements (*Hows*), established the Target Goals and identified the relationships between the *Hows* (Correlation Matrix), determined the technical specifications you'll need (*How Muches*), and rated your probability for achieving them (Probability Factor). Now you are ready to analyze the relationships among these factors and determine if the *Hows* will help you achieve the *Whats*.

The Relationship Matrix is located in the center of the QFD model. It is the means for analyzing how each *How* will fulfill each *What*. It identifies which *How* best fulfills all the *Whats*. The Relationship Matrix is located in the center of the QFD model. Figure 8-1 shows its placement.

THE RELATIONSHIPS BETWEEN
HOWS AND *WHATS*

When there's a relationship between a *How* and *What*, the *How* will ultimately satisfy a particular customer requirement or be a solution to a problem. Relationships are determined by asking if a *How* can help achieve a *What*. Record your team's responses to each question in the Relationship Matrix, using the following numbers:

Figure 8-1.   Relationship Matrix within the QFD model.

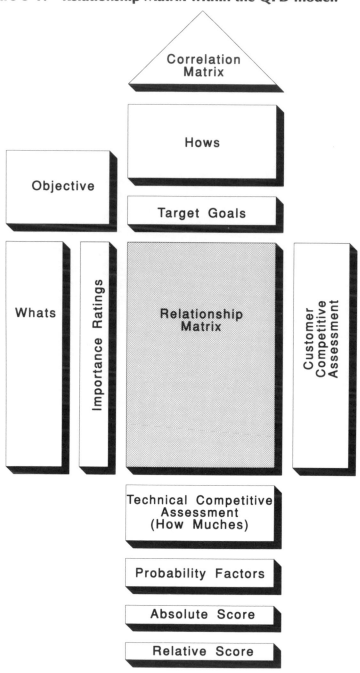

0 = No relationship
1 = Low relationship
3 = Medium relationship
5 = High relationship

Starting with the first *How*, ask the question:

Can this *How* help us achieve this *What?**

If the answer is no, enter a 0 in the Relationship Matrix. If the team responds with a yes, then ask:

Is the relationship low, medium, or high?

Proceed down the column to the next *What*, and finish the column before proceeding to the next *How*.

Caution: The facilitator must remain a neutral party. No single person can have more influence over the team's decision than the facilitator. Thus, ask only if there *is* a relationship between the *Hows* and *Whats*. Never lead the questioning to achieve the answer you want or that you think is appropriate. For example, do not ask, "There is a relationship, isn't there?"

Figure 8-2 shows how the team has entered its scores in the Relationship Matrix.

When the questioning is completed, the team should look for columns filled with zeros, indicating that the *How* does not adequately support the customer requirements. The way in which the team proposes fulfilling that requirement is not going to work! At this point, the team should reconsider the *How* and decide if it should remain in the matrix. Similarly, *Hows* that have a relationship with only a few *Whats* should be reevaluated.

Facilitator's note: Remind the team that it is being asked if a particular *How* will help achieve a certain *What*. It is not being asked *if a* What *will help achieve the* How. There is a tendency for new QFD teams to inadvertently transpose the two elements. The latter, an incorrect question, results in a greater number of significant relationships.

Figure 8-2.   Entering scores on the Relationship Matrix.

What are the important elements of Delivery?	Import. Rating (1 to 5)	Mat'l Hndlg	Prod. Sched.	Invent. Control	Ship. & Rec.
On-time	3	3	5	1	5
Quantity	3	3	5	3	5
Rec'd condition	4	5	0	0	5
Marking	5	5	1	0	3
No inspection	1	5	1	0	3
Paperwork	4	5	5	3	5
Cost & logistics	2	5	5	5	3
Absolute Score					
Relative Score					

Calculating the Cell Values

To calculate a score for each cell in the matrix, multiply the Importance Rating for the *What* by the number in the cell. To simplify entering scores, work from top to bottom and finish one column, or *How*, before proceeding to the next. Insert the product of your multiplication in the cell in parentheses; see Figure 8-3.

Determining the Absolute and Relative Scores

Calculate the column totals by beginning with the first column of *Hows*. Sum the values in parentheses and enter the sum at the bottom, in the row labeled Absolute Score.

Figure 8-3. Relationship Matrix with relative scores.

What are the important elements of Delivery?	Import. Rating (1 to 5)	Mat'l Hndlg	Prod. Sched.	Invent. Control	Ship. & Rec.
On-time	3	3 (9)	5 (15)	1 (3)	5 (15)
Quantity	3	3 (9)	5 (15)	3 (9)	5 (15)
Rec'd condition	4	5 (20)	0 (0)	0 (0)	5 (20)
Marking	5	5 (25)	1 (5)	0 (0)	3 (15)
No inspection	1	5 (5)	1 (1)	0 (0)	3 (3)
Paperwork	4	5 (20)	5 (20)	3 (12)	5 (20)
Cost & logistics	2	5 (10)	5 (10)	5 (10)	3 (6)
Absolute Score		98	66	34	94
Relative Score		1	3	4	2

Next, sort the *Hows* by highest to lowest score. For example, if there are ten *Hows*, they will be ranked 1 through 10. The *How* with the highest score is ranked 1, next highest 2, and so on. In our example, the four *Hows* are ranked 1 to 4. Place these Relative Scores in the appropriate row beneath the Absolute Scores. Figure 8-3 shows the matrix with Absolute and Relative Scores.

If two Relative Scores are the same, the facilitator asks the team:

Which *How* should logically occur first?

Typically, one *How* should logically occur before the other. The team selects the order and continues. If it cannot decide, choose the leftmost *How* and move on.

A REALITY CHECK

When the scoring is complete, the facilitator should walk the team through the newly ranked *Hows*. We call this a "reality check." Beginning with the *How* that has a relative score of 1, ask the team if it makes sense to accomplish that *How* before the others. Move on to the *How* with a relative score of 2 and repeat the question. Continue the process for the entire list of *Hows*.

Observe whether there is a logical sequence to the *Hows*. If so, congratulations; you have done the QFD matrix correctly. If there is no readily discernible pattern, then the team should reevaluate the *Hows* and decide whether other *Hows* need to be developed.

9

Strategic Applications of QFD Three Case Studies

In today's quality-minded consumer world, partnerships and strategic alliances are important for everyone's long-term survival. In many cases, these matches occur naturally owing to similar interests and beliefs, or complementary products and services. However, did you ever wonder why your company deals with a certain customer?

Do some of your customers consume 80 percent of your company's resources yet contribute to only 20 percent of its revenue? Have you ever wondered how sales gets some of the customers it does or, more important, why?

For many organizations, earning or losing new business is determined by the quality of proposal they submit. Some are faced with a paradox: New business is won by the proposal department. Better proposals require better staffing, yet the high cost of responding to proposal requests is a major factor in sales. How does an organization determine the right balance between size, cost, and quality?

Strategic application of QFD helps uncover logical solutions to this type of problem. The most surprising fact to most companies is that the solutions already exist within the company. Chapter 6 mentioned how QFD uses the collective knowledge of your entire staff to develop solutions to virtually any problem. No outside company or consultant knows your business better than your organization. QFD simply provides you with a way of extracting everyone's experience.

This chapter contains three case studies. We have selected tough problems to which QFD helped find simple solutions. They are problems we are asked to help with repeatedly. To protect the anonymity of our clients, names have been eliminated. However, they have agreed to share their matrices, in an effort to help you benefit from their experience. We hope these case studies will give you ideas about how to use QFD for your specific issues.

QFD CASE STUDY 1: IMPROVING SALES

A service-based company wanted to improve its ability to gain high-quality customers. The company services all of the United States and has branch offices in approximately twelve countries around the world. Although thousands of businesses use this company's service, a significant amount of its revenue comes from large electronics manufacturers.

The company's managers wanted to make sure that they properly used the resources they had to grow the business. However, during company growth, they recognized that different customers required different levels of support. In the early days, the nature of the business was singular. As it matured, the managers began questioning whether this was still true and if not, why not. Therefore, they wanted to develop a system to help them understand that a change had occurred. If a system could be created to help them understand why certain customers required more attention than others, could it also help determine this probability before the prospect became a customer?

We were hired to help facilitate a QFD meeting to address this problem. The company scheduled a meeting for when its entire sales staff of thirty people would be available at corporate headquarters. The meeting was conducted with these thirty plus approximately fifteen other key leaders representing all corporate functions. The total meeting time for this group was approximately three hours.

This case study illustrates a very simple application of

QFD. In an effort to keep this example simple, some of the QFD rules discussed earlier in the book have been bent. As you read this case study, we think you will find out why this was done and the benefits that were achieved.

QFD FOR PERFECT CUSTOMER CRITERIA

Very few companies have what we refer to as customer criteria: a list of qualities that a company thinks constitute an excellent customer. As simple as the idea may sound, few companies take the time to analyze new or even existing customers. Not all customers are the same, but have you ever wondered why?

For example, why does one small customer require a large percentage of a staff engineer's time, while a larger, major-revenue-producing client requires only slightly more effort? Quite often organizations lack a way of determining ahead of time who will be a good customer and who will require considerable resources.

We have developed a process to determine Perfect Customer Criteria. The process can help you quickly analyze the impact new or existing customers will have on your business. It helps produce significant savings by identifying customers that will fulfill your company's long-term strategic business plans. Where appropriate, some companies have used the process to rationalize removal of some from their customer base.

This process is very easy to do and usually takes just a few hours. It uses a cross-functional company team which may include salespeople, customer service staff, and upper management. Since your sales staff is your funnel for new customers, they should participate. Salespeople who do not participate will not buy into the criteria, and likely will not use them to the same extent as others.

DETERMINING THE *WHATS*

Figure 9-1 shows the simple QFD matrix used in this case study. The Objective Statement simply asks, "What are the

Figure 9-1.   Perfect Customer Criteria matrix.

No	(Whats)	IR	A		B		C		D		E	
	What are the important qualities of an excellent customer?		**Customer Number** A B C D E									
1	Good match of our product to their needs	5	5	(25)	3	(15)	4	(20)	5	(25)	4	(20)
2	High demand for our product or service	4	4	(16)	2	(8)	5	(20)	5	(20)	3	(12)
3	Financially sound	3	4	(12)	3	(9)	5	(15)	5	(15)	3	(9)
4	Ability to pay bills on time	2	5	(10)	2	(4)	2	(4)	4	(8)	2	(4)
5	Reputation for being good to work with	1	2	(2)	1	(1)	3	(3)	4	(4)	1	(1)
	Absolute Scores		65		37		62		72		46	
	Relative Scores		2		5		3		1		4	

* IR=Importance Rating

important qualities of an excellent customer?" Unlike for most QFD applications, we initially limited the number of *Whats* to five, so as to force the company to develop a concise list of items that everyone will remember easily. (This is especially important for the sales staff, who may have to make a quick mental comparison of potential customers and criteria.)

To develop the *Whats*, the team was asked, "What are five qualities of an excellent customer?" To avoid limiting the team's thinking, the facilitator asked the members to design the *perfect* customer: "If you were to design the perfect customer, what would it be like?"

The team discussed many qualities, however, for the purpose of this exercise, they were required to list only the top five. The final list was as follows:

1. Good match of our product to their needs
2. High demand for our product or service
3. Financially sound
4. Ability to pay bills on time
5. Reputation for being good to work with

When the list was finalized, the team ranked the items in order of relative importance. Again, for this application, we modified the basic rules for assigning Importance Ratings to require that each *What* have a unique Importance Rating. This limitation encouraged greater discussion. The Importance Ratings were as follows:

5. *Good match of our product to their needs.* Good customers were a result of meeting needs with the right product. If the need was not there, nothing else mattered. For the company to grow, it needed to match up with companies that needed the type of services and products it offered.

4. *High demand for our product or service.* The customer not only needs the product or service but needs a lot of it.

3. *Financially sound.* The customer has to be able to pay for the products or services. Financially strong companies typically are well-managed companies.

2. *Ability to pay bills on time.* Cash flow is vital to any organization. It is important that the perfect customer pays its bills on time.

1. *Reputation for being good to work with.* The technical nature of the company's products and services requires a significant customer interface. The company's current customer base included clients that are good to work with.

Note: When the team first started this process, it originally put "large corporations" as its No. 1 item, thinking that large companies use more products and are financially sound. However, as the discussion progressed, the team realized that this was not necessarily true. If a large corporation had no need for the product, then size was irrelevant. Even if the customer is large and its demand high, it must first be financially sound. Validation of this was the fact that many medium-sized companies had demands that far exceeded some larger customers and they also had better payment records. "Large corporation" was removed from the list and substituted with "financially sound."

FILLING IN THE *HOWS*

The team next turned its focus to the *Hows*. For this application of QFD, the *Hows* were easy to create, because they were new or existing clients. For the initial test and evaluation of this system, the company randomly selected five customers, giving each a letter on the matrix.

With the customers entered on the matrix, the team began assigning values to the Relationship Matrix cells: 0 = none, 1 = low, 3 = medium, 5 = high. The cell values were calculated, column totals summed, and the Absolute Scores entered, followed by the Relative Scores. The results were that Company D best fit the Perfect Customer Criteria, followed by Companies A, C, E, and B.

In reviewing its findings, the team consensus was that the matrix did indeed numerically represent the order and differences among the customers. Past experience with these customers confirmed the matrix results. For example, Company D had an absolute score of 72 points. In contrast, Company B scored 37 points, approximately half that of Company A, the second choice. In support of these findings, members of the team confirmed that dealing with Company B was much more demanding and required significantly more effort to support. Similar feelings were conveyed about Company E and the enormous amount of work it required as compared with the revenue it generated.

FIELD TEST

With completion of this initial phase, each salesperson was given a copy of the matrix and asked to fill in the names of ten top prospective customers. (Not working in teams does go against QFD philosophy; however, it was necessary for this particular exercise.) Then each was given time to work the matrix individually. This was to demonstrate how the QFD matrix could be a simple tool for identifying potential perfect customers.

The Importance Rating scales used in this exercise would give a company a total Absolute Score of 75 if it had a high relationship to each of the *Whats*.

$$(5 \times 5 = 25) + (4 \times 5 = 20) + (3 \times 5 = 15)$$
$$+ (2 \times 5 = 10) + (1 \times 5 = 5) = 75$$

The salespeople reported how many of their prospective customers scored 60 or higher (60 represents the top 20 percent). Each salesperson had at least one company scoring that high; however, most revealed that eight out of ten prospects scored below 38. To their amazement, this was less than half the Perfect Customer Criteria!

The results in this process are subjective numbers, or each salesperson's opinion of the prospective customer, according to what he or she knows about the customer. A low Relative Score does not mean the sales staff should stop calling on the prospect. However, the process helped focus these sales efforts in a more profitable direction.

EVALUATION OF THE PROCESS

QFD in its simplest form is a tool to promote communication. Using QFD to establish Perfect Customer Criteria helped this company define the qualities that make up an excellent customer. It gave the sales staff a systematic way to convert individual perceptions about customers into statistical information that the entire organization could use to make strategic business decisions. Sales managers could now analyze potential customers and prioritize their resources to their best advantage. Most important, the sales staff now had a highly effective means of filtering out undesirable business.

As mentioned earlier, this company depended heavily on winning new business by responding to requests for proposal (RFPs). In the past, a salesperson's perception of importance determined if the company responded to an RFP. Oftentimes, a desire to push the RFP through was largely influenced by an incentive plan. If someone was having a poor year, winning a large RFP could help make the numbers. As a result, these business decisions did not always support the strategic thrust of the organization. Over the years, this resulted in bad relations, perceived poor quality, and loss.

The Perfect Customer Criteria changed the paradigm for the company. The sales staff became the initial filter for profitable new business. Now, if an RFP is received, it must pass through the standard qualifications. The Perfect Customer Criteria allows everyone in the organization to understand and recognize good business. As a result, sales no longer has to wait for corporate decisions on whether to pursue new business, and the company no longer wonders why sales even submitted the prospect for consideration.

QFD CASE STUDY 2: IMPROVING THE RFP PROCESS

This case study shows how one major aerospace subcontractor used QFD's problem-solving ability to develop a better way to meet customer needs.

For many organizations, new business is determined by responding to requests for proposal (RFPs) or requests for quotation (RFQs). Companies spend valuable time and resources responding to the detail many of these proposals request. Some organizations believe that winning 10 to 20 percent of the proposals they respond to is normal and a very good average.

Our client did not feel satisfied with the percentages that had become acceptable in the industry. Rather than respond to many and win few, our client wanted to respond to few and win many. Its goal was to develop a system that would result in winning 75 percent of all RFPs responded to. The company decided to use QFD to break this industry paradigm and achieve its goal.

Another important reason driving this company's need for a new RFP system was what the company referred to as its burnout factor. Its current process was not very effective because it wasn't really a systems approach to RFPs. Every RFP was processed in a slightly different manner. Thus, employees worked long, hard hours trying to ensure that all aspects of an RFP were properly completed. Turnover was high and tenure in the department was usually less than one year. The proposal department was continually growing, with no end in sight. Once considered administrative and sales overhead, the proposal department was now becoming a major cost center with budget demands mushrooming. Lacking an effective means to prioritize, coordinate, and gather all internal materials for the responses, employees rushed the RFP to make the deadline. Often, one individual or department could jeopardize the RFP by sitting on vital information. And the quality of RFPs varied considerably because there was no effective way to respond to each item.

The company's CEO asked us if QFD methodology could help solve the RFP response problems. The company sanctioned an initial QFD session, with a team of fourteen representing all the organization's functions. The matrix, shown in Figure 9-2, was completed in a single four-hour session.

THE OBJECTIVE

The team's Objective Statement was, "What are the important qualities of the RFP process?" The team began by discussing the current process of response to RFPs. This defined what was involved and what was needed. As a result, numerous *Whats* were developed, categorized, and sorted. The team felt that there were three phases to the RFP process:

1. Quality decision criteria
2. In-system cost
3. Postdelivery

Quality Decision Criteria

The team recognized that an excellent RFP system would initially determine if the RFP matched the company's strategic business goals and objectives. Quite often, responses to RFPs were determined by the amount of lobbying done by salespeople or managers with special interests. To screen and evaluate RFPs before dedicating resources to a response, there would need to be a filter system. The team referred to this as bid/no bid.

Figure 9-2. RFP system matrix.

No	Whats (What are the important qualities of the RFP process? — Request for Proposal)	IR	Contin. Imprvt.	Mfg.	Sales Mktg.	Parent Comp.	Finance	Purch.	Quality	Engnr.	Pres.	Legal	R&D	Sec.	Flow Chart Proc.	Custom	Supplier	TQM Teams	TQM Phil.	Safety
	Quality Decision Criteria																			
1	Quality Decision Criteria	5	1 (5)	1 (5)	5 (25)	(0)	(0)	(0)	3 (15)	3 (15)	(0)	1 (5)	1 (5)	(0)	5 (25)	5 (25)	1 (5)	3 (15)	3 (15)	1 (5)
2	Bid/no bid	1	(0)	(0)	(0)	(0)	(0)	(0)	(0)	(0)	(0)	(0)	(0)	(0)	(0)	(0)	(0)	(0)	(0)	(0)
3	**In-System Cost**	2	(0)	(0)	(0)	(0)	(0)	(0)	(0)	(0)	(0)	(0)	(0)	(0)	(0)	(0)	(0)	(0)	(0)	(0)
4	Product	5	(0)	(0)	3 (15)	(0)	(0)	(0)	5 (25)	3 (15)	(0)	(0)	3 (15)	(0)	5 (25)	5 (25)	3 (15)	3 (15)	5 (25)	3 (15)
5	Strategy	3	(0)	(0)	(0)	(0)	(0)	(0)	(0)	(0)	(0)	(0)	(0)	(0)	(0)	(0)	(0)	(0)	(0)	(0)
6	Regulatory/legal	2	(0)	(0)	(0)	(0)	(0)	5 (10)	(0)	(0)	(0)	(0)	(0)	(0)	(0)	(0)	(0)	(0)	(0)	(0)
7	Technical aspects	4	(0)	5 (20)	5 (20)	(0)	(0)	(0)	5 (20)	5 (20)	(0)	(0)	(0)	(0)	5 (20)	5 (20)	5 (20)	5 (20)	5 (20)	3 (12)
8	Logistics (customer sched.)	4	(0)	(0)	5 (20)	(0)	(0)	1 (4)	5 (20)	1 (4)	(0)	(0)	5 (20)	(0)	5 (20)	5 (20)	5 (20)	5 (20)	5 (20)	1 (4)
9	Value pricing	3	(0)	(0)	(0)	(0)	(0)	5 (15)	(0)	(0)	(0)	(0)	(0)	(0)	(0)	(0)	(0)	(0)	(0)	(0)
10	Approvals	1	(0)	(0)	(0)	(0)	(0)	(0)	(0)	(0)	(0)	(0)	(0)	(0)	(0)	(0)	(0)	(0)	(0)	(0)
11	Delivery	5	(0)	(0)	5 (25)	1 (5)	1 (5)	1 (5)	1 (5)	1 (5)	1 (5)	(0)	1 (5)	5 (25)	5 (25)	5 (25)	3 (15)	5 (25)	5 (25)	1 (5)
12	Method or packaging	4	(0)	(0)	5 (20)	(0)	3 (15)	1 (4)	(0)	(0)	3 (12)	3 (15)	1 (4)	5 (20)	5 (20)	5 (20)	1 (5)	(0)	5 (20)	(0)
13	**Postdelivery**	5	(0)	(0)	5 (25)	(0)	(0)	(0)	(0)	(0)	(0)	(0)	(0)	(0)	5 (25)	5 (25)	(0)	5 (25)	5 (25)	(0)
14	Award/no award	4	(0)	(0)	(0)	(0)	(0)	(0)	(0)	(0)	1 (5)	1 (5)	(0)	(0)	(0)	5 (20)	(0)	3 (12)	(0)	(0)
15	Debriefing	3	(0)	(0)	(0)	(0)	(0)	(0)	(0)	(0)	(0)	(0)	(0)	(0)	(0)	(0)	(0)	(0)	(0)	(0)
16	Documentation	2	(0)	(0)	(0)	(0)	(0)	(0)	(0)	(0)	(0)	(0)	(0)	(0)	(0)	(0)	(0)	(0)	(0)	(0)
	Absolute Scores		5	25	150	5	20	38	85	59	22	25	49	45	160	180	80	132	150	41
	Relative Scores		17	13	4	18	16	12	6	8	15	14	9	10	2	1	7	5	3	11

How Legend:

Continuous Improvement	Purchasing
Manufacturing	Quality Function
Sales & Marketing	Engineering
Parent Company	President
Finance	Legal

Research & development	Supplier
Secretarial	Total Quality Management Teams
Flow Chart Process	Total Quality Management Philosophy
Customer	Safety

In-System Cost

Once an RFP passed the initial decision criteria, its technical requirements could be evaluated. The *Whats* in this category consisted of processes to further assess and determine the merits of the RFP, as follows:

- *Product*. Determination of how the request matched the type of products the company provided.

- *Strategy*. Determination of how the request fit into the company's business strategy. Was it work the company wanted to pursue, or was the company moving away from that field?

- *Regulatory or legal*. Elimination of work not of interest to the company, owing to regulations such as those of the U.S. Environmental Protection Agency. Other work carried too high a liability factor.

- *Technical aspects*. Evaluation of specific technical aspects of the project was done once earlier levels of filtration were accomplished.

- *Logistics*. Consideration of customer delivery schedules. Could all necessary resources be assembled properly in time to meet customer demands?

- *Value pricing*. Determination of costs and pricing issues.

- *Approvals*. Coordination of legal, costing, technical, and corporate approval. Properly informing all parties of all aspects of the proposal and coordinating these efforts were difficult tasks.

- *Delivery*. Timely delivery of the RFP response as well as the product. An excellent RFP system would have to properly analyze and determine all elements that contribute to giving customers what they want when they want it.

- *Method or packaging*. Determination of customer packaging and method for delivery requirements.

Postdelivery

Once the technical requirements of the RFP are fulfilled and the company notified if its bid is accepted or rejected, evaluation of the result can be performed.

• *Award/no award*. Follow-up on bid. Responding to RFPs often requires significant time and resources. Losing an RFP provides an opportunity to improve. An excellent RFP system would provide for follow-up to understand why an RFP was won or lost.

• *Debriefing*. A way to capture the information learned in the award/no award phase. Proposal department staff convene to discuss what worked in the process and what didn't.

• *Documentation*. Capture and use of follow-up information. Understanding why RFPs were won or lost is of little value if the information is not available for future reference. The outcome of the bid and the information identified in the debriefing session are documentation to be filed in the company's file.

THE QFD MATRIX

The QFD team developed a variety of *Hows* to fulfill its list of *Whats*. Many of the *Hows* involved departments; others were processes and philosophies. They were as follows:

Continuous improvement
Manufacturing
Sales and marketing
Parent company
Finance
Purchasing
Quality function
Engineering
President
Legal
Research and development
Secretarial
Flowchart process
Customer
Supplier

Total Quality Management teams
Total Quality Management philosophy
Safety

This was the company's first application of QFD. To keep it simple, the team decided to concentrate on QFD's problem-solving capabilities. *How Muches* (quantifiers for the *Hows*) were not used. The team also believed that, in order to create an excellent RFP system, it should attempt to fulfill all the *Hows*; therefore, there were no Probability Factors. And because this was a strategic application, unique to this business, the competitive assessments were not used.

After completing the Relationship Matrix and assigning Relative Scores, the team did a reality check of the ranking of the *Hows*. A summary of their reality check is provided below.

Customer

The item that surfaced as No. 1 to help improve the RFP system was of little surprise to anyone. The QFD process told the company that no single item would do more for improving its RFP process than getting face-to-face with customers to learn about their needs. Yet the current system did virtually nothing to break down barriers. The new system would have to provide a way of allowing the organization to listen firsthand to its customers' needs. The system to accomplish this would be Quality Function Deployment, or QFD.

Flowchart Process

When flowcharting the process was first offered by a team member, few colleagues felt it had much value; however, it was allowed to remain on the list. This *How* proved to be important. Through detailed discussions, the team realized that flowcharting the current process would help identify non-value-added functions and steps that caused delays. It also would give the team a benchmark against which to measure all steps in their process and improve its flow.

Total Quality Management Philosophy

Earlier that year, the organization had adopted Total Quality Management and continuous improvement philosophies. The RFP process was considered as another business process. And like any other process, continuous improvements could streamline the process and make it more efficient. The company's philosophy would thus prove vital to its development and implementation of a new RFP system.

Sales and Marketing

These two functions offer the first line of contact with customers. Effective communication with customers can provide valuable information for responding to an RFP. The QFD team felt that these functions could play a vital part in the RFP process, yet the current system had sales and marketing personnel only randomly gather customer requirement information. There was no formal method to share and disseminate information to people writing the proposal. In the new system, sales and marketing would, through well-defined process steps, be responsible for supporting the overall success of the RFP operation.

Total Quality Management Teams

The company had recently formed some Total Quality Management teams. These teams would play an important role in analyzing and improving the functions that contributed to developing RFPs.

Quality Function

Under the Total Quality Management philosophy, the company was transforming its quality department into quality consultants. Each department would now be responsible for its own quality. The quality department would not provide "inspection" functions; rather, it would assist other departments in developing their use of statistical techniques, design of experiments, Pareto analysis, and so on. The new RFP system would require all departments to develop new measurements for their portion of the process. The quality function would provide training and assistance to these departments as needed.

Supplier

The company recognized that its product quality was no better than its poorest supplier. Meeting higher demands from customers was going to require active participation from suppliers and subcontractors. As a result, subsequent QFDs were conducted to determine the important qualities of the company's supplier development system.

Engineering

The engineering function was a vital part of the company's aerospace business. The changing business environment required ever-increasing value-added services for customers. Engineering provided the technical expertise for quoting all RFPs. The better it understood the customers' needs and applications, the better it could determine the effort required to fulfill them. As part of this process, engineering would further use QFD when responding to future RFPs.

Research and Development

Many applications required R&D to produce new products, processes, or techniques that fulfill customer requirements. Like engineering, R&D must be able to effectively communicate with the customer to fully understand those needs and requirements.

Secretarial

Receipt of incoming RFPs, coordination of internal documents, and publishing the finished RFPs require a significant contribution from the company's secretarial staff. The QFD process brought to everyone's attention the need to keep this group informed of key information. Like all the other functions, Secretarial Support was an important part of the RFP process.

The QFD matrix helped the team determine that all eighteen *Hows* had some relationship to fulfilling the goal of a new RFP system. As the Relative Scores indicate, some of the *Hows* have a more direct impact. When subsequent QFD sessions to develop the RFP process were held, each of the *Hows* were listed as *Whats* and were used to help create the new system.

CONCLUSIONS

By using QFD, the team realized that the RFP process was, in fact, another business process. Up until this time, no one considered it a process or thought about using continuous improvement tools as they had been applied to manufacturing. After using QFD, the company began applying these rules and techniques to RFP. This was a milestone for the organization.

QFD helped the company realize that responding to customer needs is one of its more critical business processes. The RFP process determines how new business fits and supports the company's long-term strategic goals. It also serves as a filter through which all new work must pass. For the company to grow, decisions regarding RFP must be stable and repeatable.

Note: Our Perfect Customer Criteria (described in Case Study 1) was adapted by this company as well. Before any RFP or RFQ was submitted by sales, it had to pass minimum selection criteria. As a result, the number of RFPs and RFQs submitted dropped dramatically.

The RFP system developed here became a sophisticated and highly effective business process for this aerospace subcontractor. The first year the new RFP system was used, the company achieved a win ratio of just over 50 percent of the jobs bid on. Although this was off from its target goal of 75 percent, the company was already getting more business by quoting on less than half the number of jobs quoted the previous year.

The new RFP system served the company well. It was able to secure 20 percent more business using half the effort. Before bidding on a job, the company knew its probability of getting it. As the company further developed its use of their RFP system and added Customer Competitive Analysis, its win ratio steadily increased. New business fit long-term strategies. By using QFD, the company gained a marketing edge over its competition.

The new RFP system help solved the burnout problem as well. Responding to only half as many RFPs meant the proposal department was less rushed and could better focus on its work. Although employees still occasionally put in long days, it became the exception rather than the rule. Also, the proposal department added improvements to its response system so as to analyze each proposal and determine department interaction and responsibility. This dramatically reduced response delays. With QFD used on the front end of an RFP, each department could identify its contribution, required quality level, and deadline for completion.

QFD CASE STUDY 3: DEVELOPING A TRAINING PROGRAM

This case study shows how an insurance company used QFD to develop a new training program. Customer service was extremely important to this company's daily operation. Its customer service department consisted of over 100 employees, who handled thousands of customer telephone calls daily. Knowledge of product, processes, and procedures was a skill that had to be taught before anyone could assume a customer service desk.

We helped this company benchmark its performance as part of its Total Quality Management directive. With the staff as part of the assessment team, it was discovered that better training for this department could prove valuable. Already trained in the use of QFD, management decided to use the process to develop some new training programs and revise some existing ones.

The Objective

The QFD involved approximately fifteen people representing all functions within the organization. The team's Objective Statement was "What are the important qualities of training?"

The team developed several *Whats*. (Owing to the competitive nature of this business, several *Whats* and all the *How Muches* have not been shown, as per the agreement to use this QFD matrix.) The *Whats* were as follows:

1. Timeline—evaluation and implementation
2. Screening—hiring
3. Designated trainer
4. Ongoing in-house training
5. Overview of company orientation
6. Outside education

The Approach

The team developed the following list of *Hows* that might accomplish the qualities it felt were important in training:

Employee checklist
Training manual
Testing
Job descriptions
Corporate training
Job knowledge
Prior experience
Trainer evaluation
Cross-training
Outside services
Attitude
Manager evaluation
Executive evaluation
Trainee evaluation

See Figure 9-3 for this matrix. The following are explanations of what each *How* meant.

Figure 9-3. Training Development matrix.

No.	What are the important qualities of Training? (Whats)	H O W S — IR	Empty Checklist	Training Manual	Testing	Job Desc.	Corp. Training	Job Knowlrg.	Prior Exper.	Trainer Eval.	Cross Training	Outside Services	Attitude	Mrg. Eval.	Exec. Eval.	Trainee Eval.
1	Timeline - evaluation/implement	5	5 25	5 25	5 25	1 5	3 15	1 5	1 5	5 25	1 5	1 5	3 15	5 25	3 15	3 15
2	Screening - Hiring	4	1 4	3 12	5 20	5 20	1 4	3 12	3 12	3 12	0 0	1 4	3 12	5 20	0 0	1 4
3	Designated Trainer	4	3 12	5 20	5 20	3 12	5 20	5 20	5 20	1 4	3 12	5 20	5 20	5 20	3 12	5 20
4	Ongoing In-House Training	3	5 15	5 15	5 15	3 9	5 15	5 15	3 9	5 15	5 15	3 9	5 15	5 15	3 9	5 15
5	Overview of Comp. Orientation	2	1 2	5 10	1 2	3 6	0 0	1 2	1 2	5 10	0 0	0 0	3 6	3 6	0 0	1 2
6	Outside Education	1	3 3	0 0	3 3	3 3	0 0	3 3	5 5	1 1	1 1	5 5	5 5	5 5	3 3	5 5
	Absolute Scores A-1		61	82	85	55	54	57	53	67	33	43	73	91	39	61
	Relative Scores		7	3	2	9	10	8	11	5	14	12	4	1	13	6

Competitive Assessment	Empty Checklist	Training Manual	Testing	Job Desc.	Corp. Training	Job Knowlrg.	Prior Exper.	Trainer Eval.	Cross Training	Outside Services	Attitude	Mrg. Eval.	Exec. Eval.	Trainee Eval.	Total
Absolute Scores A-2	5 / 305	4 / 328	4 / 340	4 / 220	3 / 162	4 / 226	4 / 212	4 / 268	1 / 33	3 / 129	5 / 365	4 / 364	3 / 117	5 / 305	100% / 3376

Probability Factor	Empty Checklist	Training Manual	Testing	Job Desc.	Corp. Training	Job Knowlrg.	Prior Exper.	Trainer Eval.	Cross Training	Outside Services	Attitude	Mrg. Eval.	Exec. Eval.	Trainee Eval.	Total
Absolute Scores A-3	5 / 305	3 / 246	3 / 255	4 / 220	2 / 108	4 / 228	5 / 265	4 / 268	4 / 132	5 / 215	5 / 365	5 / 455	5 / 195	4 / 244	104% / 3501

| **Final Relative Scores** | 3 | 7 | 6 | 10 | 14 | 9 | 5 | 4 | 13 | 12 | 2 | 1 | 11 | 4 | |

How Legend:

Employee Checklist	Job Knowledge
Training Manual	Prior Experience
Testing	Trainer Evaluation
Job Descriptions	Cross Training
Corporate Training	Outside Services
Attitude	
Manager Evaluation	
Executive Evaluation	
Trainee Evaluation	

• *Employee checklist*. The team felt that a checklist would allow employees to assess their own skills and provide improvement guidelines for gaining certain positions in the company.

• *Training manual*. The company already had a good training manual. However, to achieve the level desired, improvements would be required, including more use of graphics such as actual photographs of computer screens. In addition, more specific measurements for both students and instructor would have to be developed.

• *Testing*. In the past, testing was always performed on the student, not on the process by which the student was taught. The training process included the set of courses, their sequence, and their timing relative to time spent performing certain job functions. With the Total Quality Management philosophy, the test would now focus on the process. Student test scores should indicate how well the training process works and where it needs to be improved.

• *Job descriptions*. Many team members initially thought that having a more detailed job description might help achieve better training. A detailed discussion followed and, to find out its importance, the *How* was left on the list.

• *Corporate training*. During the benchmarking process, the company discovered that many employees did not really understand how the company started, who its founders were, or how other divisions of the company operated. Corporate training was viewed as a process that could give employees valuable background information while teaching the executive leadership's business values.

• *Job knowledge*. This *How* was provided as a means of measuring how well each employee knew and performed the job.

• *Prior experience*. Earlier experience proved to be a characteristic of many successful employees. Experience within the industry, especially at similar companies, was especially valuable. This *How* was a way of measuring that value.

• *Trainer evaluation*. Trainers were viewed as a critical part of the process. In the past, test scores only represented how much the student retained. In the TQM environment, tests could provide feedback on how effective the trainer and training methods were.

• *Cross-training*. In the past, cross-training was virtually nonexistent in the company. Cross-training would allow employees to handle a variety of positions.

• *Outside services*. The company recognized that there were external training skills that it would continue to need. This *How* included consulting, seminars, and specialized training programs unique to the industry.

• *Attitude*. Although attitude is difficult to measure, it was never formally quantified. Only during postinterview debriefings would interviewers give their perceptions of a potential employee. Yet in determining the qualities of successful employees, attitudes always ranked high. For the new training system, the team would develop better measurements to quantify this attribute.

• *Manager evaluation*. Becoming a manager in this company was no simple task. Experience, training, and excellent people skills were important prerequisites. Only after many years of demonstrated ability did employees become managers. Managers had to have the ability to recognize how new employees would fit into their department. Because of this, it was important to have new employees receive manager approval to attend training.

• *Executive evaluation*. This *How* refered to upper management's evaluating employee performance before and after training.

• *Trainee evaluation*. Measuring the trainee's performance after training remains an important aspect of the training process. This *How* referred to measuring learning success. The results from this evaluation were used to determine the most effective trainer style and trainer methods.

The team worked through the Relationship Matrix and determined the Absolute and Relative Scores. "Manager evaluation" became the *How* that would accomplish more *Whats* than any other item. It was followed closely by "testing" and "training manual."

COMPETITIVE ASSESSMENT

The QFD team then gave the list of *Hows* to marketing to learn whatever it could about how key competitors trained their employees. Marketing was to research each specific *How* within thirty days. Upon completion, the marketing department gave its perceptions of how well the best competitor addressed the *Hows*. In some cases, marketing had quantifiable data; other times, it had only its best guess. Nevertheless, the assessment values represented the best of the best. Absolute scores (A-1) were multiplied by the Objective Values, or *How Muches*. These scores were entered in the row labeled Absolute Scores (A-2). The values were totaled horizontally for a sum of 3,376—the benchmark standard representing 100 percent achievement.

PROBABILITY FACTORS

The QFD team next entered its perceptions of the ease with which the company could achieve each *How*. The Absolute 1 scores were multiplied by these Probability Factors, and the new scores were entered in the row marked Absolute Scores (A-3). These scores were also added horizontally for a sum of 3,501, which, when divided by Absolute 2 scores (3,376), indicates a 4 percent increase over the best of the best.

CONCLUSIONS

"Manager evaluation" remained No. 1. The process was easy to do and helped the company achieve its objective. The former No. 2 *How* was "testing." However, using Probability Factors, it fell to No. 6 because testing was a relatively new subject for the company.

"Attitude" rose to No. 2 because the company had the basics in place to determine this. Its Probability Factor said that it would be easy to add measurements to get quantifiable results.

When the team completed its calculations, it immediately discovered that the new training system would be only approximately 4 percent better than the best in its class. For the amount of time and money involved, the team felt that this small gain was not adequate. Rather than quit, however, the team improved its *How Muches* to achieve approximately a 10 percent gain.

Thus, QFD served this organization well. Long before it had invested money in developing a new training program, the company recognized the potential problems. Inexpensive adjustments were made in the development cycle and, as a result, implementation and completion went smoothly. To no one's surprise, the new training program was very successful.

10

Conclusion

You are finishing a book that can affect your competitive position in the marketplace, both today and in the future. QFD is a powerful tool with broad application: design, strategic planning, problem solving, product or service development. We have simplified QFD so that it can be used by both technical and manufacturing businesses.

If you're new to QFD, you now have a new tool to add to your business toolbox. If you are an experienced QFD user, we hope we have expanded the way you think about QFD and that you will consider using it more. Solve your next problem through QFD and compare the results to other methods. Don't limit QFD to design and manufacturing; let it permeate your entire organization.

By reading this book you have learned how to identify exactly what it will take to satisfy your customers' product or service requirements. You have seen how you and the competition are perceived by customers. You know the minimum standards you must reach and how to achieve them. You have established technical specifications that will raise you above the competition. You know the resources available and the probability of providing those specific quality demands. You have accomplished all this without designing a single part or committing to a single service. This is the power of the QFD methodology!

Index

[Page numbers followed by *n* indicate material in footnotes.]